AROUND HAUNTED MANCHESTER

A Book of Source Material

by
Peter Portland

Published by AMCD (Publishers) Limited
PO Box 182, Altrincham, Cheshire, WA15 9UA
MMII

Other Titles from AMCD in this Series:
Around Haunted Croydon by FD Stewart 1989
Surrey Ghosts Old and New by FD Stewart 1991

Front Cover: Wythenshawe Hall, Manchester
Rear Cover: The John Rylands Library, Deansgate, Manchester.
The Old Parsonage, East Didsbury. The Cage, Lyme Park.

Around Haunted Manchester by Peter Portland
First Published by AMCD (Publishers) Limited MMII xxxi. x.
AMCD (Publishers) Limited, PO Box 182,
Altrincham, Cheshire WA15 9UA, England

Email: web@amcd.co.uk   Web: www.amcd.co.uk

ISBN: 1 897762 25 9

Printed by: The Commercial Centre, Hollinwood, Oldham. Absit omen.

CONTENTS

ACKNOWLEDGEMENTS

Grateful Thanks to:

Peter Bamford, *Cheshire and Chester Archives and Local Studies, Cheshire Record Office*

Mrs Brenda M Folds, *The Tabley House Collection*

Dr George Fildes, *Manchester Museum*

Alan Garner *for oral variants to the tales of Nell Beck and Firbank the Gamekeeper*

Karen Humphries, *Mansion and Old Hall Manager, Tatton Park*

John V Knott, *Archivist, Smithills Hall & Park Trust*

Daniel Parkinson *of www.mysteriousbritain.co.uk*

Jonathan Schofield, *Blue Badge Guide, Manchester Ghost Walk*

The Staff of Didsbury Public Library

The Staff of the Manchester Central and Local History Libraries

Emma Marigliano and the Staff of the Portico Library & Gallery Manchester

The Staff and Porters of the John Rylands University Library, Deansgate, Manchester.

The Manchester Museum, The University of Manchester

Oldham Local Studies and Archives

LIST OF ILLUSTRATIONS

WARNING TO THE READER

Ghosts, poltergeists and boggarts are serious business: don't meddle with them. But if you must persist, and do come across the odd visitant, here are a few simple tests you might like to apply:

No self-respecting ghost of any antiquity, be it from Manchester, Cheshire or Lancashire, will speak anything but dialect. If the spectre is older than Anno Domini 1500 it won't even be speaking a form of the language that you will recognize as English. If you understand it, it's modern. Try these simple translation tests:

'Jeppe Knave Grave: Ki fust decolle come laron'
Grave of Jeppe the Lad, who was beheaded as a thief.

This is a nice mixture of Norman French and some form of English *(from Whalley in Lancashire)*. Probably before 1300. Beware, it may be a lawyer's ghost *(difficult and expensive to lay)*. Next test:

'Queme quyssewes then that coyntlych closed
His thik thrawen thyghes with thongs to tachched;'
Fair cuisses also cunningly covered his thighs,
that were thick and brawny, and were tied with thongs.

If your ghost speaks like that *(thong-tied)* you have probably got to deal with a Cheshire Elemental *(one of the worst sort)* from the 1370s, in full armour, as evidenced in Sir Gawain and the Grene Knight. Prepare for decapitation at the least.

If on the other hand its utterances are as follows, you are dealing with a Lancashire Boggart with a sense of humour, from the 1870s:

'There's noan so mony folk at likes to go deawn yon lone at after delit, aw con tell yo !'

Not many people like to go down there alone after daylight, I can tell you.

At least, as attested by Edwin Waugh in his *'Grizlehurst Boggart'* tale from *'Lancashire Sketches.'*

Finally, any self respecting 1580s' Catholic priest, even if only of the screaming skull variety, should be able to manage Latin - not strangulated English Latin, but proper Catholic Church Latin:
'Tristitia vestra vertetur in Gaudium !'
Your sorrow shall be turned into Joy.

Brythonic and Early Welsh Ghosts may also be encountered. Seek expert help.

Also, note carefully the costume. There is far too much sloppiness in reports. *'Elizabethan'* is not good enough. The skill in identifying and dating Elizabethan ghosts lies in looking at the ruff, i.e. the ornate white lace starched collar. From the 1550s to the 1580s fashionable men and women wore a small ruff about two inches (5cm.) wide, close to the head. From the 1580s onwards many people wore a much larger variety, styled "Head on a Platter" and reaching onto the shoulder. Starch was provided by the 'Lords and Ladies' plant, with the usual allergic reactions.

The fashion for ruffs continued in England until the early 1600s, when long plain white collars replaced them. The larger ruffs were expensive to make and keep clean - hence only for the rich. There were also double ruffs (banned in 1562, to no avail) and 'standing ruffs' - worn by women around the edge of the neckline at the back of the dress. So, small ruff - probably a pre-1580s ghost. Big ruff, probably post-1580s. No ruff, but vaguely Elizabethan looking - probably Henry or Mary Tudor.

You should also try to see if any men are wearing wigs. These were pretty much obligatory in the period from the 1670s onwards as Louis XIII went prematurely bald. To be seen without one was a cause of great social unease. They were removed when duelling (with swords). There were also civilian and military variants, and they continued in fashion until 1795, when a tax on hair powder effectively put paid to the style.

Remember: five minutes with a good period costume guide can be worth an hour fiddling with heat-sensitive devices in a dimly-light beer cellar.

THE BRERETON DEATH OMEN

There was at Brereton a pool, since drained, variously called Bagmere, Blackmere or Brereton's Lake which presaged the death of one of the Breretons by sending up tree roots or trunks:

'HERE is one thing exceeding strange, but attested in my hearing by many persons, and commonly believ'd. Before any heir of this [Brereton] family dies, there are seen in a lake adjoining, the bodies of trees swimming upon the water for several days together....

Supposing them true, [these omens may be the work] of the holy angels that guard our persons, or of devils who, by divine permission, have powerful influence on this lower world.'

Camden, Britannia. 1586

'That black ominous mere
Accounted of those, that England's wonders make;
Of neighbours Blackmere named, of strangers, Brereton's Lake,
Whose property seems far from reason's way to stand;
She sends up stocks of trees, that on the top doe float,
By which the world her first did for a wonder note."

Michael Drayton, Poem of Polyolbion, 1622

The pool of that name is still extant, now an SSSI, still with some water and reed beds. Perhaps the trees are still lying there, remnants of forests overwhelmed at the last glaciation.

FOREWORD

MANCHESTER: A PSYCHIC LANDSCAPE HISTORY

Manchester is a psychic curiosity: it lies at a psychic crossroads.

To the South is the natural witching barrier of the River Mersey, and beyond that the fertile plains of Cheshire - Cheshire of the Brythonic Cornovii safe for a while against Rome in their Wrekin hillfort. From Cheshire Lindow Man, his stomach full of a last Celtic psychotropic meal, swam back into our consciousness, a leathery corpse, after two millennia in the peat brown water. Heavily Puritan in the Civil War, Cheshire bred Bradshaw, the judge who sentenced Charles I to be beheaded.

To the North is the higher moorland of Lancashire, of the Federated Brigantes, with their Goddess of fertility, healing and wisdom, Brigantia. Their warrior queen Cartimandua, clever enough to assess the imperial Latin might, handed over Caradoc to the Romans and became both wealthy and arrogant as a consequence. Here the Celtic sacrifice was a girl, thrust into Red Moss at Bolton perhaps two thousand years ago, unearthed in 1943, but since then lost in quiet oblivion between Birmingham Medical Department and Bolton.

Catholic Lancashire with its long train of purgatorial souls, and the Pendle witch hunts. A place where the Gunpowder Plot could fester; the route which would bring Bonny Prince Charlie swinging into Deansgate in 1745 - that last throw of the Celtic Catholic world against the Hanoverian satanic industrial mills.

Away to the East lie the Derbyshire Dales: closed, inward-looking, subterranean, with their limestone caves and lead-mines. Yet these mines penetrated as far as Alderley Edge, and allowed deep stabling and repose to Arthurus, Rex Quondam et Futurus, his wizard Merlin, his 999 knights and their steeds, accoutered to ride out again, at England's time of utmost peril.

And to the West ? To the west lies Roman Chester, and beyond that the unruly Welsh. There we here the faintest low bell, carried on the centuries, of the primeval Enochian language of the Angels heard by John Dee, the Elizabethan Conjuror of Angels. For Dee came to Manchester (1586-1604), and commissioned the first physical map of this City from Christopher Saxton. That map of course vanished, but it is not the only etheric guide to our kind of deep triangulation......

Oral history is one guide. It is often cited as a source for legends and for ghost stories. It must however be one of the weakest modes of transmission, far inferior to the written, which itself is subject to misinterpretation. We know for example that the Latin Mass was celebrated in Lancashire almost continuously for perhaps one thousand four hundred years, until it was replaced by the English Mass in 1965. Yet the amount of Church Latin that has entered common parlance is small: hocus pocus [hoc est corpus], pater noster, ave Maria.

Manchester had only just printed its first book *(1585 - a lost Catholic tract)* when ghosts began to appear locally in print: in 1615 we find John Trundle publishing 'Newes out of Lancashire, or the strange and miraculous revelacon of a murther [murder], by a ghost, a calf, a pigeon etc'. The etc is worrying. When John Dee came to Manchester he brought his library with him - probably the best in Manchester at the time. These he lent out, and the flavour of his collection is given by the following: De Praestigiis Daemonum *(on Demonic Tricks - one of the first books to considers possession an illness)*, Malleus Maleficarum, *(Hammer of Witches)* the Flagellum and the Fustis Daemonum *(The Scourge and The Cudgel of Demons)*. These are early guides to the state of mind of Manchester and its magistrates, to later explode in the Lancashire Witch Trials of the early 1600s.

A GHOSTLY WILL

For the first local account of local ghosts we go back to a
legal instrument dated 1518, the tenth year of the reign of King
Henry VIII and set in Lancashire. This account survived only
in an 18th century copy, so perhaps the antiquarians had
already got to it by then:

*'Be it known to evry Christen man to whom this present
wrytinge shalbe read or understode that wee Sir Olyver Breres,
Sir Hugh Folly, Priests [there follow the names of twelve other
witnesses] witnesseth and testfyeth on our trothe that one John
Pilkington of Whittle in the woods spake with the Ghoste of one
James Parker deceased divers years before.'*

This looks like intriguing material - attestation by two
priests and 12 other witnesses. Perhaps too good to be true,
because the real reason seems to have been a contested will.
James Parker's two daughters, Jone and Jenet, *(the text is not
completely clear)* appear to have been defrauded of their
inheritance by one George Parker. The ghost pointed the
finger, and the lost will, together with 'evidences, deedes,
scroules and muniments as was in ye keepinge of the said
George' were delivered to the two girls. This looks like a good
family squabble over inheritance, in which some mummery
and literal shroud-waving disgorged the relevant papers, and
sorted out the matter in equitable fashion.

The astrologer John Dee's associate and dark guide, Edward
Kelly, is said to have raised a recently dead man in the
graveyard of St Leonard's Church at Walton-le-Dale in
Lancashire. It is sometimes affirmed that Dee was also present.
This must have been grisly work - Kelly is said to have had his
ears cropped at Lancaster Assizes for some transgression, and
wore a black bonnet pulled down low to disguise these marks
of a criminal past. The spirit was summoned at midnight, re-
entered its corpse and was persuaded to divulge the location

of a treasure it had buried in its lifetime. Dee, of course, died poor '......oppressed with extreme poverty', in the words of one early biographer.

TOO MANY GHOSTS

The problem with ghosts in Britain is not their absence, but their large numbers: Robert Roberts' in his book A Ragged Schooling (1976) states of Salford before the First World War:

'Few houses in our district stood vacant for longer than a fortnight before ghosts got in. Irish neighbours usually gave warning of the new tenants, then children heard of it *"......there's summat stirrin in that empty No.7. Raps an moanin." '*

Certainly this book could have been much longer: almost every pub in Manchester, and most of the Libraries, are haunted. Indeed Mass Observation in the 1940s concluded that one in four of the population had had some kind of supernatural experience. It would be an interesting project to correlate those experiences to films and television - UFOs seem to be fading into the past *(Close Encounters of the Third Kind was 1977)*; Poltergeists are also a little passé *(The Exorcist, 1973)*.

Indeed Tabley Old Hall is said to have given rise to the film The Ghost goes West (1936) - the story being that an American offered to buy the Old Hall in its derelict state from Cuthbert Leycester-Warren. This gave the writer Ian Hay the idea of the ghost going along, and getting out in the US when the door was finally opened. Whatever the influences on popular sensibility, one finding seems clear - every 30 years or so, the old ghost stories are dusted off and re-issued in new clothes as new books, new films and now websites.

EARLY FOLK TALES

At the base of the folklore of much of Manchester and Lancashire lies the work of John Roby (1793-1850) and his Traditions of Lancashire. Born at Wigan, he was a partner in the bank of Fenton and Roby. He apparently had great facility with numbers and mental calculation, but could also mimic people and perform ventriloquism. He seems to have had a powerful religious conversion in 1844, concomitant with a strong sense of sin and worthlessness, which led him away from the Church of England towards the Chapel. He spent much of his later life lecturing, particularly at 'Mechanics Institutes.' He visited both Scotland (1823) and the Lakes (1832) as well as much of the Continent (1837-40). He died in June 1850 on his way to Scotland to gather fresh folklore material.

His Traditions of Lancashire sold out in its first year, went to three editions in his lifetime, and was admired inter alia by Sir Walter Scott. It underpins many of our present current ghost stories, though perhaps with not so much accuracy or attribution that we might like. He also published plays and poetry. His Traditions was noted for the 200 or so characters which he created - these seem to have little or no connection with any factual characters, but were rather fictions. He was also credited by a German reviewer in The Story of Rivington Pike with creating *"the only authentic tale of demoniacal possession that the English have."*

Roby was an early believer in comparative anthropology - that myths were the same worldwide. *"Odin and Jupiter are brothers"* in his striking phrase. He also picked up the strange stories of John Dee, his time in Manchester, though Roby's story of Dee, the buried treasure and its guardian spirit, is in fact rather weak. Roby is also responsible for putting into wider circulation a number of ghost stories, including that of George Marsh at Smithills and the Wardley Hall Skull *(covered below)*, as well as the Eagle and Child legend illustrated in the arms of the Stanleys of Derby and Alderley. As we shall see, his tale of Boggart Hole Clough is a complete fabrication.

SOUL CAKES

There were and are still local customs associated with the dead that certainly maintain belief in spirits. Spirits in almost every culture demand to be fed, as in life. Soul cakes seem to be very ancient indeed in Britain: there is a reference to these in 1574 by a witness at a law suit that she had gathered soul cakes in her childhood on All Souls' Day. Even further back, it seems likely that Lindow Man two thousand years ago in the early Roman period was given the burnt portion of some form of psychotropic soul cake (containing mistletoe) as a last meal before his triple death.

Soul cakes seem to have no modern currency, though there are still *'Hot Cross Buns'* now available all year round - not just in Holy Week. They too had their own pedestrian song - if any one can recollect it. Even in Henry Green's time at Knutsford in the 1850s the consumption of soul cakes seems to have been restricted to small hungry boys - *'At the present day and in this neighbourhood, a child's sport....'*

The Soulers too had their song, as they went around requesting food, but only imperfect and probably censored versions have come down - a few lines from that cited in 1819 in Ormerod's Cheshire give the flavour:

'You Gentlemen of England, I would have you to draw near
To these few lines which we have wrote, and you soon shall hear
Sweet melody of music all on this ev'ning hour
For we are come a souling for apples and strong beer.'

Most end with a blessing on the *'master and mistress, their cattle and store, and all that lies within their gates.'* Suppressed is of course any reference to prayer or intercession for the souls of the faithful departed in Purgatory. Doubtless before that, the Christian church had also vigorously suppressed any pagan elements in the middle ages.

The Catholic Church continues of course to say masses and prayers for the dead; reductions in time to be spent in Purgatory for particular dead souls through indulgences are also possible by special prayers at All Souls. But All Souls' Eve has now become the American Halloween, with 'trick or treat' and other imports - or perhaps they were English customs taken to America by English settlers ? All Souls' Eve was also a time for divination: nuts or apple pips were heated in the fire to see if they exploded or burnt with a steady glow - the results showing the temper of the person they were said to typify. Useful, if marriage was being contemplated.

There were local constraints on the dead, as on the living. Ghosts may not walk from Christ's Nativity (25 December) to Twelfth Night (6th January- the coming of the Magi). Nor are spirits allowed to be abroad in Holy Week (immediately before Easter). Their allotted time is of course All Hallows Eve.

SPIRITUALISM: *'Who dun blowed out dem lights?'*

Given that the business of mediums is to contact and be contacted by the spirits of the dead, it is surprising that most books of ghost stories take no account of the influence of Spiritualism on common beliefs - particularly since its rise in the 1840s and legalisation in 1951.

Spiritualism is conventionally dated from the 'Rochester rappings' in New York State of 1848. Three female American mediums arrived in Britain in the period 1852-53, and had considerable success. Newspapers were founded - notably the Yorkshire Spiritual Telegraph (1855) and the British Spiritual

Telegraph (1857), which put spiritualist ideas into circulation.

The North of England seems to have attracted a strong spiritualist following, in part because many of the concepts were already in circulation: apart from uninterrupted Catholicism, there has been Swedenborgianism, and Behmenism (followers of the German mystic cobbler Jakob Boehme). There were also Owenites - followers of Robert Owen, who founded the co-operative movement. At the same time there was the ferment of the 1848 revolutions across Europe, and interest in mesmerism, herbalism and phrenology.

The American Shakers also originated in Manchester: Mother Ann Lee, the founder of the Shakers was born and christened in Manchester in 1736, and her American movement recruited in Britain. David Richmond, who was a key link in bringing spiritualism to Britain was a Shaker, a vegetarian and a teetotaller. He is credited with bringing 'table manifestations' to England.

But there was a radical social angle to Northern spiritualism, sometimes called 'plebeian spiritualism' or 'spiritual communism': Thomas Paine and Martin Luther appeared at one séance - and some disappointment was expressed by participants that a revolutionary should appear with a religious reformer. Robert Owen, very old by the time of the Spiritualist heyday, believed that spirits were hurrying forward the time when socialist and co-operative ideals would dominate the world - he was later to communicate the principles of modern spiritualism from beyond the grave (see below). By 1901 Spiritualism and séances were attracting Labour Party members such as Keir Hardie, but its heyday was probably over by then.

Manchester had its own spiritualist paper - The Two Worlds, founded in 1887 by Emma Hardinge Britten (1823-1899) in Manchester, at 'The Lindens, Humphrey-street, on Cheetham

Hill', and still published today. Britten learned her mediumship in America in the 1850s, and disseminated it worldwide. At her instigation, the Inaugural Conference of the Spiritualists' National Federation was held on the first Sunday in July 1890 in the Co-operative Hall, Ardwick, Manchester.

Britten, was also the medium through whom in 1871 Robert Owen is said to have communicated the basis of the Seven Principles of Spiritualism, which were later to be adopted by the Spiritualists' National Union as the basis of its religious philosophy. One of her last books was Ghostland of 1897.

Today, a century after her death she is almost forgotten, and Manchester University and Central Library do not appear to have a single book by her (apart from bound copies of 'The Two Worlds'). These make rather thin reading, marred by incongruous advertising ('magnetised cod liver oil'). They have little on ghosts per se, the principal entries being poetry. Some of the articles have been taken over straight from American sources - not so alien, given the enormous impact that the American Civil War had on the Cotton industry in Manchester. One line, which probably needs no attribution as to speaker, may stand for the flavour:

'Miss Sallie, who dun blowed out dem lights in yo'r room an in de parlour ?'

Who indeed. Reader, read on.

FAMILIARS

PHANTOM CAT

The Phantom Cat of Swinton.

Swinton

A cat to begin with. Cats are psychic, uncanny animals. They represent the feminine persona. They glare at sights unseen by us. They have the power to appear and disappear noiselessly - particularly if, like the one in this story, they are phantoms. It starts innocently - but at three psychic boundaries: a new marriage, a new house, the Autumn as nights draw in.

> 'When my husband and I were first married, in the Autumn of 1964, we moved into the top flat of a newly converted house in Swinton, Manchester. The house had been split into two flats after the previous owner died. On three occasions, separately, and once together, we saw a cat, smallish and black, walk from the landing into the living room across to the window, and vanish.'

Now animals as apparitions are not uncommon, but it is curious that they should have an afterlife in common with humans, and should continue to behave as they did in life. The couple do not appear to have been afraid - but rather incredulous:

25

'The windows in the flat were sash, and shut, and each time this happened we were decidedly incredulous and shut all doors hastily in order to search each room thoroughly, at our leisure. On none of these occasions was there any trace of any animal.'

Now the game really begins, because the cat, in common with some other spirits, has the ability, perhaps the need to attach itself to its new owners. It is reminiscent of the poltergeist in Boggart Hole Clough which cannot be shaken off simply by moving house: it flits with you.

'The animal moved with us to another flat in London, where we saw it once, but after we bought two Siamese cats into our lives, the black one was not seen again.......'

A very catty, feminine, jealous ending to this tale. Perhaps the black cat went back to Swinton. Any recent sightings ?

PHANTOM HOUNDS

Deansgate, Godley Green, Burnley Trash, Paddy in Didsbury.

The Manchester Area is fortunate in having two tales of phantom hounds. The first is a headless black beast which propelled a man called Drabble from what was then Manchester Old Church *(now the Cathedral)* down Deansgate one day in 1825. The dog put its forepaws on his shoulders, and with tremendous force, drove him to his own house. Drabble is said to have been so terrified that he leapt into bed fully clothed and with his boots on. This hell hound was later laid to rest, bound by some spell to remain under an arch of the Bridge over the River Irwell for the canonical lease of nine hundred and ninety nine years. The Mancunians, ever canny, buried it on the Salford side, beyond running water....

The second beast was at Godley Green, and perversely has a yellow coat, and the stature of a cow. It was seen to run through the neighbouring fields and lanes, and had one extraordinary characteristic: according to a report of 1906 the beast kept pace with a Hyde fishmonger, stopping when he stopped, running when he ran. When he tried to strike it, his hand simply passed through, hitting the hedge. Finally the beast passed him, only to rush back again - the head in front, without apparently having turned around. The fishmonger was told by the local farmer that he and his family had often seen it. Middleton in his Legends of Longendale interviewed the fishmonger in 1906, and had direct confirmation of the story: *'It was no cow....It was ghost. I never want to see the thing again if I live to be a hundred years old.'*

This apparently was a not uncommon sighting - a child had also seen it, and it had kept pace with her too. She was stopped by a relative from throwing stones at it by the odd comment that it was a ghost-hound, and would tear her to pieces if she did, implying some degree of familiarity with the phenomenon or its folklore. Another lady had seen it standing by a frozen pond, and thought it might be an escaped lion from Belle Vue Zoo - its skin 'much the same as a lion's in colour'. Again the beast was seen to follow her as she backed away, only to disappear near to her house. It was said to have eyes like saucers, feet that went pit-a-pat.

The interesting point about these two beasts at Godley and Manchester is their almost magnetic attachment to their victims. Another name for this kind of phenomenon was 'Trash' in the Burnley area, said to be so-called from the splashing noise it made as it walked on large broad feet - but there is a variant 'Guytrash.' Now the Oxford English Dictionary (OED) covers Guytrash in our meaning here. But it has a strange entry under 'Guy'. It cites a meaning of 'guide' in a quotation from 1350 - but in a context peculiarly appropriate to our concerns: *'werewolf that was al her gye'* - 'the werewolf that was their only guide.' 'Trash' is confirmed as a dialect word for splashing through mud, but also has another sense: a leash attached to a dog. These links may be no more than coincidence, but they seem to point to a group of meanings, perhaps confused in the popular etymology.

Some of the staying power of this legend probably comes from the tale of The Hound of the Baskervilles by Sir Arthur Conan Doyle, but Guytrash also manages to creep into Jane Eyre by Charlotte Brontë: on first seeing Mr Rochester's dog in the lane at dusk she says

> *'I remembered certain of Besse's [her nurse] Tales wherein figured a North-of -England spirit called a 'Gytrash'; which in the form of a horse, mule or large dog haunted solitary ways and sometimes came on belated travellers.'*

Trash too resembled a huge dog with saucer eyes. It had matted shaggy hair. 'Trash' too had no substance and could not be touched, only seen. If followed, 'Trash' would retreat backwards with an unblinking gaze attached to its pursuer, but if your attention wandered for even a second, it vanished. A further variation was The Shrieker or Shriker, also Skryker - an invisible entity manifested by a shrieking noise.

Burnley Trash, the Manchester, and the Godley Green hounds may all be similar to Black Shuck in East Anglia - explainable perhaps as forms of ball lightning, running along leys. This might account for the strange matching of pace, their immense power, and the curious noise effects. They are of considerable antiquity - the first recorded instance in England seems to be 1127 at Peterborough. There is now a wide literature on black dogs, and also a number of websites - one sponsored by Elgood's Black Dog Beers.

C. Elsie Mullineux says that a similar dog - '*Owd Tratcher*' - was still to be seen (1990s ?) at Pennington Flash (a large lake) at Leigh. At Walkden near Bolton she mentions that there was an area with two wells at the junction of Hodge Road and Walkden Road - the wells each had their individual qualities, with one better for brewing tea, the other for washing clothes. This was also a spot for gypsy encampments. More ominously, there appeared here the phenomenon, in the form of a fearsome hound with green eyes, much used by parents to terrify children.

There is a less menacing dog to be found in Didsbury, South Manchester - at the junction of Spath Road and Holme Road. It was here in 1957 on a clear moonlit night that a local policeman saw a dog walking across the lawn of an old house. It went behind a large tree, but then vanished. Intrigued, the policeman went back during the day to look at the spot - only to find a small moss-covered animal gravestone inscribed "Paddy. Died 2 September 1913."

FLETCHER MOSS

VICTORIAN GHOSTHUNTER

Didsbury

There are fashions in ghosts and hauntings, just as there are fashions in clothes, tattoos, rings, piercings. Fletcher Moss, the antiquarian of Didsbury in the 1890s had some very modern remarks to make about ghosts:

> 'In olden times priests or parsons would have been called in to lay the ghosts. Nowadays people are losing faith in the powers of the priesthood; they want the drains inspected and the rent reduced....'

Moss had a fine collection of folk-lore, and it is full of the supernatural. At times he is unwilling to identify the exact location of hauntings - lest he should find himself 'liable at law for damages incurred by depreciation of the property'. Thus he does not specify the house near to Didsbury in which no tenant would remain long. But note how the action of the story is set at the canonical sixty years in the past:

> 'The front windows are all broken, and if they are mended they are soon broken again. There is a melancholy pit in the orchard, and the whole place looks lost and lonesome. No one will stay in the house, for they say a man named Aaron Warburton, who lived there sixty years ago, "comes again" and will persist in showing new tenants how he did that deed that ends all other deeds'.

Moss does identify one Didsbury residence: The Swivel House - or at least that was once its name. Its occupier was one Sam Dean, an elderly bachelor who had made his fortune out of 'swivels' - small hand-looms for making tape or other thin material. Sam Dean died, and his fortune was found to be missing.

The Old Parsonage, Didsbury

Swivel House was sold, but a ghost began to walk there: not that of innocent Sam Dean, but rather a beautiful lady - too beautiful, in the clothes of another period, red shoon, powdered hair, a kerchief tucked into her bosom. This visitor never spoke, but glided from room to room with a dry rustle of her silk gown. There were those who said she was an old sweetheart of Sam's, who had taken the cash.

In Moss' time (1890s) this spirit had long since ceased to walk, though 'about seventy or eighty years before' (so, in the 1820s) a newly arrived housekeeper had been told she could have anyone to sleep in her room she wished, if she was afraid of the ghost....Moss adds a curious little coda to his tale: starting with the innocuous but completely mid-leading statement: 'The Deans were a very old and respectable family in the neighbourhood....' he proceeds to give what may be his own view of events at The Swivel House:

'About a hundred years since one of them [the 'respectable' Deans] was hanged in chains on Stockport Moor for having murdered his wife at the instigation of one Sal Fogg, a lady of easy virtue who lived at Cheadle. An old man says that his grandfather when a boy had gone to see the murderer's body on the gibbet and thrown a stone at it..........'

Some folk customs are the better for passing into oblivion.

The Swivel House was rebuilt and enlarged. In the course of this there was found in the chimney stack a small secret chamber with a table and chair and some chicken bones. Common consent had it to be a priests' hole from the time of the Catholic persecution. The name of the house was changed and changed again, till the fine lady, or perhaps just a lady in finery, ceased to walk. It seems to no longer feature in local knowledge.

Small Earthquake At The Old Parsonage, Didsbury

Fletcher Moss also mentions the Old Parsonage at Didsbury, where he lived for many years. The house itself is secluded, set back from the main road. It looks towards St James' Church and churchyard, and over the park now named after Fletcher Moss, towards the upper reaches of River Mersey. Its date is uncertain - perhaps no earlier than the Commonwealth of the 1600s, though its position on a bank well above the regular Mersey floods suggests that the site may be much more ancient.

The house is long and low, and the garden has now reached that peak which our forefathers could only imagine in their mind's eye when they laid it out. There is a neat Victorian porch with trelliswork. Inside the ceilings are low, and in Fletcher Moss' time there was no ventilation, drains or damp course. Various repairs had been effected with gravestones, which might alarm the more tender; human remains were regularly turned up in the garden.

But Fletcher Moss is remarkably silent on any apparitions at the Old Parsonage: servant's bells ringing in the small hours are tracked down to rats in the bell-pull wiring - these are coming in from the Cock Inn stables next door. An unearthly screaming in his mother's bedroom turns out to be the wind howling through a broken window pane. He sees and seizes a dark figure in the garden, but it is the local policeman checking that all is well.

The most that Fletcher Moss will subscribe to is an indeterminate presence:

'Probably hundreds of times I have been awakened out of sleep and heard someone coming upstairs, stealthily and quietly, step by step; heard the doors open and shut; have gone after them

and found nothing.......The dogs know when the ghosts are about. Three months since (December 1896) there was an earthquake, and the bed shook under me, wakening me up. I merely muttered to myself "Well I wonder whether that is a bogie or an earthquake" and instantly went to sleep again, forgetting all about it until the next morning when in the train going to town, the passengers were all talking of the earthquake....'

This earthquake (which came in two shocks) was at about 5:30 in the morning, and was felt across the whole of England and parts of Wales.

THE DISAPPEARING BOGGART

BOGGART HOLE CLOUGH
Blackley, Manchester 1827-2002

A Boggart Churning Milk.

This is surely a name crying out for a ghost. The Boggart
was a name to frighten children and adults - a bogeyman,
spectre or hobgoblin which haunted wastes and isolated
places. Gatley had its resident boggart - the Black Pit Boggart
near to Hob Bridge (Hob is another name for this nasty
character - there are nine hob place names which are related to
goblins in Cheshire). There was a Boggart Lane in Didsbury -
now under Didsbury Park. There are plenty of other examples
- Dodgson, the place name expert, notes at least six in Cheshire
- one associated with an ancient tumulus. There is a *'Boggart
Hole'* in Oldham and another in Derbyshire. Curiously there
are none listed for Lancashire. Ekwall omits Boggart Hole
Clough from his 1922 study of Lancashire place names, so
depriving us of a date. The strange reason for this will become
clearer below.

Boggart Hole Clough is a deep romantic valley in Blackley,
North Manchester. In 1896 an estimated 40,000 people
gathered here to hear Kier Hardy, one of the founders of the

modern labour party, speak. In 1906 it was the location of a Suffragette Rally where Mrs Pankhurst spoke. Today it is one of Manchester's principal leisure parks, with many sports on offer. The City has lapped around it, but it still retains a wild character, suitable for orienteering.

The tale is told by Roby in 1827 in his Traditions of Lancashire of the farmhouse of George Cheetham subject to the mischievous attacks of one such boggart, which caused havoc and destruction at night. But on other occasions it was sweetness itself: milk was churned into butter, pans scoured without the agency of human hand. "Rest ! What is rest? Boggart knows no rest!" was the complaint of its disembodied voice. Roby's tale even has a piece of folk etymology: there was knot in the wood one of the floorboards; the children would insinuate a shoehorn into it. The Boggart would expel it in such a way as to strike the head of whoever put it there. Hence Boggart Hole. This was called *'lakin wi't' Boggart'* [playing with the Boggart].

No remedy was found against this supernatural visitation. Particularly annoying was the nightly walk of someone in clogs. In a fury, the farmer ordered his family to pile all their belongings onto the wagon. As they were about to depart, a neighbour came by and remarked *'Yer leavin' th'owd house'?'* From a milkchurn on the wagon a deep preternatural voice replied for the whole family:

> *'Ay, Ay neighbour, we're flittin.' '[G]od rot thee !'* says the farmer, *and if I'd known thou'd been flittin too I wadn't ha stirred a peg! Nay Nay, it's no use.... we may as weel turn back again to th'owd house as be tormented in another not so convenien*t.'

The family had realized there was no point in trying to flee their visitant, and began to unload their possessions. But the Boggart is also said to have taken the farmer's words to heart -

there was no point in flittin with the family to less convenient quarters. Over time his own lakin' slowly decreased and finally ended. Though people say that he still likes a good joke, and can be heard laughing in the depth of the woods. Sophisticated observers will probably detect something of the poltergeist here - the disruption at night, the attachment of the boggart to the family or perhaps to one member of it.

John Roby 1793-1850

Now this is a good tale, told with much accretion of detail. When Roby was compiling Traditions of Lancashire he was in touch with another author, Croften Croker author of '*The Fairy Legends and Traditions of the South of Ireland*'. Croker had published a tale of a "*Cluricane*" - a kind of leprochaun, called '*The Haunted Cellar*'. A reviewer of Croker's book in the Literary Gazette of 1825 happened to mention a similar tale from Yorkshire. The temptation was too much: Croker grafted a good Yorkshire tale onto a strong native Lancashire stock -

still alive today. The word 'lakin' is apparently the clincher - this is a Yorkshire word, not often found in Lancashire. The ensuing story was included by Roby and versified by Tennyson in 1842 in his English Idylls, probably giving the story further impetus and veracity.

It is also surprising to discover that the very name 'Boggart Hole Clough' may be a fabrication: Edwin Waugh does a pretty good hatchet job on the whole story in his Lancashire Sketches of about 1850. Talking of fairies or the 'feeorin' - fearful things - he cites a letter of June 18th 1851 he received from a friend,

> *'an ancient and desolate looking house standing in this valley and known as 'Boggart' or 'Fyrin-Ho' Kloof' (The Glen of the Hall of Spirits)......I was dining some short time ago with a legal gentleman who informed me that he was at a considerable loss, a few years back how to describe the place in question [Boggart Hole Clough], having to prepare some notices to be served on trespassers. On referring to the title deeds of the property he found that a family of the name of Bowker had formerly occupied a residence situated in the Clough.... Designated Bowker's Hall. From them the place took its name, and as such he described it.'*

It is fairly astonishing to see the Boggart and the placename both vanish into thin air - all the more since both are now so well established in the public mind. But.....the same story occurs across much of Europe. Roby cites a Spanish parallel, and seems aware of the Danish version He does not allude to the fact that in the Danish version the same verb- 'flitter' is used and with the same meaning.

Already by 1843 Samuel Bamford in Passages in the Life of a Radical had caught the Boggart Hole craze, and, in a macabre short story was citing it as a suitable venue on St John's Eve for a herbalist to gather fern seed in an old skull for a potent love charm to aid a love-sick youth. The magic proves however too strong and strange creatures emerge from the bracken. The herbalist and his assistants flee in terror. Although the maiden is lured to the bedside of the youth, he dies from the shock of what he has seen.. The herbalist is prostrated for three days, his assistant goes stark mad, and the skull, by now gibbering independently, has to be reinterred at the crossroads whence it had come - evidently a suicide. Strong stuff, literature.

Longsight Boggart

By the 1880s the Boggart genre was producing humorous dialogues, in the form of a Christmas penny leaflet by the Rev. JA Atkinson, Rector of Longsight (a poor working class area of Manchester), entitled The Boggart O' Longsight. Other Boggarts are mentioned in this account (Clegg Hall and Boggart Hole Clough), as well as intriguingly, 'a Lady in silks between Fairfield and Ashton' who disappears when approached.

Do Boggarts still exist ? Probably their very name has disappeared from common usage. Axon says in 1899 that a phrase still heard occasionally then was 'Aw'm comin' too, like the Clegg Ho' [house] Boggart." This quotation has the added pleasure and aggravation of setting the events at a completely different spot in Lancashire - Clegg House or Hall. Waugh has a story of the Grizlehurst Boggart, laid for its annoying habits by being buried with a cock run through with a 'stoop' [stake]. We shall go no further.

Nonetheless, it has been reported that the Boggart Hole Clough area in the last century attracted occult ceremonies. This may be on a par with the attraction of the Druid's Circle at Alderley - a Victorian Folly, now of immemorial reverence.

Be that as it may, the only real spirit today appears to be the produce of the Boggart Hole Clough Brewing Company, who have adopted the Boggart and its tale. A full and interesting version can be viewed at: *http://www.boggart-brewery.co.uk/*

It is in fact a mule, having another slightly weird Boggart Cat Tale grafted onto it. Roby would probably be appalled, but a run from 1827 to 2002 is not to be sniffed at.

A LITERARY GHOST
(1830-1880)

ALDERLEY EDGE: THE LEGEND OF ELLEN BECK

Base of the Old Cross at Alderley

Alderley Edge is fortunate in possessing not one but two tales which command interest and respect. The first, that of the 'Wizard', is too well known to need repeating. There is however a second, which meshes with the tale of the Wizard, but yet, despite its apparent greater documentation, has rarely been recounted or examined in any detail. It is that of the unfortunate servant girl Ellen Beck.

This story has several written sources, which claim to draw on local oral tradition. Some of the oral informants claim direct knowledge of the events, which must be set in the late 1740s or 1750s. The tale probably begins with the record of an Eleanor Beck, daughter of Peter Beck being christened on 13 February 1721 at Wilmslow, though given the tendency for family first names to repeat, this may not necessarily be our 'Nell Beck.'

THE PRINTED VERSION

The main published source is the slim volume 'Alderley Edge and its Neighbourhood' which was published anonymously in July 1843, though it was by the Hon. Miss L[ouisa] D[orothea] Stanley, daughter of the first Lord Stanley. The foreword to this expressly states that it is 'A short description and account of .....such lore as has been collected in years past from the oldest and most intelligent of the Inhabitants...' This seems to suggest not a contemporary collection by the author, but a delving into older sources - this may be the Stanley Genealogical Manuscript of her father, using material collected in the 1830s.

Miss Stanley had access to tales from a 'John Finlow, who lived to the age of 96 or 97, and died in 1828. He had a remarkable memory and much acuteness.' This places his birth in 1731-32. Mention is also made of John Potts 'who used tell many anecdotes' for example about the arrival of the Young Pretender's forces in 1745 at Alderley, when he too was young boy, and so probably contemporaneous with John Finlow. But for the Ellen Beck story it is to a Thomas Ridgway that the author turns.

'Thomas Ridgway, speaking of this tradition (i.e. The Wizard Legend) used to tell of a young woman who lived as a fellow servant with him in his youth at Fallows Hall - her name was Ellen Beck. Ellen was wont to say, that she had seen the Iron Gates not far from the Holy Well, and returning with some person for the purpose of examining them, they were not to be found. She used to describe them as two large iron folding gates.*

[A footnote continues] *This Ellen Beck's was a sad history - a Tragedy of real life, and alas it is to be feared, not a very rare one. It would seem from the stories of two old

The Wizard Inn at Alderley Edge

men from whose recollections many an annal of the Parish has been collected, (Finlow or Potts, and Ridgway) that they had both known her well. One of them had been her fellow servant at Fallows Hall. She afterwards lived at the Old Hall at Alderley.

Ellen had a lover, who probably trifled with her affections. There was another young woman in the house of whom she was very jealous. One day, as she sate upon his knee, she asked if him if he would marry her, and pressed him to fix a day; he put her off and refused. She then entreated him to give her poison. "Nay," answered he, "I love thee too well." Poor Ellen however, found the poison for herself. Her happiness and peace he had poisoned sufficiently. She was found a lifeless corpse.

> *"And there were strange reports about,*
> *But still the coroner found*
> *That she by her own hand had died,*
> *And should be buried by the wayside*
> *And not in Christian ground."*

And the body of poor Ellen Beck rests in a quiet grave where the grass grows green above her, under a hollow bank near the Brindlow Wood, in one of Armstrong's fields. It is a farm now tenanted by William Hulme. Ellen's Grave is well known by all the people thereabouts - any one will point it out. Some years ago three upright stones marked the spot, but one Dewsbury took them up and threw them into the lane - they are no longer to be seen.'

Curiously, the author is silent on the servant who led Ellen to her fate, though by implication it might have been Ridgway. There is also the suggestion in the term 'strange reports' that the coroner's verdict should perhaps have been murder, rather than suicide.

LEDGERS: THE PRINCIPAL SOURCE

The second version, or rather versions occur in the Stanley Genealogical Book, also compiled in the 1830s by the First Lord Stanley. It mentions a version of the story collected not from Ridgway, but from John Finlow. This account differs in many respects, placing the events actually on the Edge, at Armstrong's Farm - still there today - rather than at Fallows Hall. It mentions that the girl was pregnant - not explicit in the Miss Stanley account. The Stanley book is in many respects telegraphic - a series of quick jottings:

> *'Armstrong's Tenement A young woman by name Ellen Beck, a servant at the place, being with child by a fellow servant poisoned herself on his refusing to marry her. The coroner's verdict was filo (sic) de se and she was buried in a field of this farm not far from the Brimlow land under a hollow bank.'*

NELL BECK'S GHOST

A further later source is the semi-anonymous 'T.J.' - probably Thomas Jarman, in the Stockport Advertise Notes and Queries, Volume I of 1881. Jarman was a Stockport merchant. He confesses that he is not from the area, since he cannot decipher the location given as the fairly straightforward 'Brundla' - ' I am not sure of the spelling of this word, but real old Alderley people will readily know which place is meant; if it be wrong, I should feel pleased to be informed how it should be spelt...' Brundla must be the modern Brynlow on Artists Lane, Stanley's Brimlow, and a name current even in the Domesday Book - 'Bruno's Hill'

The T.J. account continues: his informant and a group of boys were walking together at dusk, 'they all having hold of each others' hands. They said they would have a toll-bar, and that everyone who passed must pay them a toll'.

'Tolling' was in fact an old custom which was fairly widespread in England and existed in Cheshire. It occurred at a time called Hocktide - the second Monday and Tuesday after Easter. Records of it go back to at least the 1200s, and it was a time when the Court Leet (of the Lord of the Manor) met, and various rents were paid. It was also the custom for young men on the Monday, and young women on the Tuesday, to exact tolls from passers-by by closing roads. Tradition has it that the young women always collected more money than the men, since they paid the men in kisses, but themselves took only cash.

Now it is rather crucial to this particular part of the story that it seems to have occurred at a time of ceremonial significance: all leases were up for renewal; gates were open; roads closed. The young men were probably tolling for kisses. It is both pathetic and proper that Ellen Beck should therefore appear to them - 'At this juncture their pleasant sport was suddenly interrupted by the unexpected appearance of Nell Beck, who emerged from a recess by the wayside, and glided lightly before them. They all plainly saw her pass, and all saw her disappear into a bush on the other side of the road.'

Not surprisingly the boys ran in a blind panic down Artists' Lane till they reached the Cross on the present A34.

TJ contributed other tales to Cheshire Notes and Queries, and in one claims to have lived at Alderley as a child, and to have heard the story of Firbank's ghost and the cast-iron bottle. It is not clear why he distances himself from Alderley in this story.

THE STORY TODAY

In 1998 a series of local history talks were held at Alderley Edge. The author took the opportunity to ask local people if they knew where Nell Beck was buried. Although the story was still current, it was no longer possible to ascertain the location of the grave. The main source for the tale appears now to be literary: 'Alderley Edge and its Neighbourhood' though the transcription of the Stanley Ledgers of the 1830s and the entry in the 1881 Cheshire Notes and Queries was known to some. These are some of the comments:

'My Uncle S... had Armstrong's Farm, but even I couldn't tell you where Nell Beck was buried... though I know the general place.'

'One of the stones from Nell Beck's grave is located in Armstrong's Farm. J...L... had the farm. The stone had a chain on it. Perhaps he had the bull tied to it. If it came from Brindlow it had come quite a way.'
S.M. 1998

"In my family oral tradition, Nell Beck drowned herself in a marl pit (still extant) in Windmill Wood, close to where she was buried."
Alan Garner, Personal Communication, October 2002

THE STATELY HOMES

MOTIVATION AND THE LEISURE INDUSTRY

There is a strict requirement, probably many centuries old, that Stately Homes be haunted. The 'leisure industry' does nothing to quash this, and indeed ghost walks and Halloween events are often organised, based on rather flimsy accounts of hauntings.

Previous generations knew why houses were haunted: often there was a residual guilt about how property had been acquired at the Dissolution of the Monasteries in the 1530s - this kind of analysis can easily be applied to a large number of former religious houses in Cheshire. Indeed, it was noted early that many of the properties so acquired were cursed, and did not stay long in one family - see 'The History and Fate of Sacrilege' by Spelman of the 1600s. There was too a feeling that the separation of rich and poor was accentuated at this time, with many charitable endowments and doles being suppressed.

Greed as a motivation is also said to have caused the ghost of Sir John Towneley (1473-1541) to walk - in an early Tudor improvement he had enclosed or 'taken in' for his park some 194 acres of common land in Lancashire at Hore Law and Hollin Hey Clough, and his ghost was said to plaintively reproach his own family to give it back ('lay out'):

> "Be warned ! Lay out ! Be warned! Lay out!
> Around Hore-Law and Hollin-Hey Clough,
> To her children give back the widow's cot.
> For you and yours there's still enough."

This story is very curious, since the occupation was declared illegal in 1556 - but the land was then appropriated by the Crown, not reverting to the Towneley family until 1612.

COMBERMERE ABBEY

Combermere Abbey is interesting in that Fletcher Moss is almost completely silent on any haunting in 1898. The most he can summon at the end of some ten pages of text is that 'the monks come again, even to the bedside'.

It is curious that he almost completely overlooks a detailed account which appeared in the publication All The Year Round on 24th December 1870, though the date of the article and the publication (Charles Dickens and his son were the editors) makes the story rather suspicious. The tale was picked up again in Cheshire Life in December 1937, though in an abbreviated version.

This apparition was identified as the ghost of a little girl who haunts the Abbey, a former Cistercian establishment, and who by her appearance foretells the death of a member of the family of the Combermeres. The account, which is an example of early journalese, is full of complicated grammar that can only have come from much reworking of the material (paragraph three is a good example). Furthermore there are at least three shifts of speaker, with relevant emotional attributes, from Miss P---, to Lady Combermere, to the young Lord Combermere. The author states that:

> 'Miss P---, niece of Lord Combermere. often stayed at the Abbey before her marriage. One evening, Miss P--- was alone, dressing for a very late diner, and as she rose from her toilet glass to get some article of dress, she saw standing near her bed, a little iron one, placed out in the room away from the wall, the figure of a little girl dressed in a very quaint frock, with an odd little ruff around its neck. For some moments Miss P--- stood and stared, wondering how this strange little creature could have entered her room.

The full glare of the candle was upon its face, and as she stood looking at it the child began to run around the bed in a wild distressed way, with a look of suffering on its little face. Miss P---, still more and more surprised, walked up to the bed and stretched out her hand, when the child suddenly vanished, how or where she did not see, but apparently into the floor.

She went at once to Lady C.'s room, and inquired of her to whom the little girl she had just seen in her room could belong, expressing her belief that she was supernatural, and describing her odd dress and troubled face. The ladies went down to dinner, for many guests were staying in the house.

Lady C. thought and thought over this strange appearance. At last, she remembered that Lord C. had told her that one of his earliest recollections was the grief he had felt at the sudden death of a little sister, of whom he was very fond, fourteen years old.

The two children had been playing together in the nursery, running round and round the bed overnight. In the morning he was told she had died in the night, and he was taken by one of the nursery maids to see her laid out on her little bed in the "coved Saloon".

The sheet placed over her was removed to show him her face. The horror he felt at the first sight of death made so vivid an impression on him that in extreme old age he still recalled it. The dress and the face of the child, as described by Miss P--- agreed precisely with his remembrance of his sister. Both Lady C. and Miss P--- related this to the writer........'

It is unclear if a family death then ensued. A Viscount Combermere did in fact die in February 1865, so perhaps this is an echo of that event. He had an elder sister, called Penelope, who is recorded as expiring 'suddenly at an early age' by Viscountess Combermere in her memoir of her husband. Dating these events is always problematical, but it looks as her death might be placed in 1772.

The 1870 article cannot refer to the then (1870) Lord Combermere, Sir Stapleton Cotton, who lived on until 1876 when he passed away at the age of 92, having been a soldier for 77 years, and fought in 17 battles.

Perhaps the Combermeres were attracted to weirdness: on 5th December 1891 a Miss Sybil Corbett took a famous photograph of the interior of the library at Combermere Abbey. In an elaborate upright chair can be distinguished a ghostly figure, identified (but not to everyone's satisfaction), as Wellington Henry, Lord Combermere, only son of Sir Stapleton Cotton. Ghostly indeed, since he was at that moment being interred some four miles away in Wrenbury, after being run over by a horse-drawn carriage in London. The chair was said to be one in which he had regularly sat.

Sybil Corbett did not make the photo public until 1895. According to her records she had used an exposure of one hour. This would allow for someone to enter the room, sit in the chair and then leave, making a fleeting imprint on the negative. Photographic experiments at the time by Sir William Barrett of the Society for Psychical Research managed to duplicate the effect of the Combermere ghost, but no member of the household, servant or family, seemed to have the right looks or the opportunity to have posed in the chair. American spiritualists had been experimenting with 'spirit photographs' from the 1860s and were aware how easy it was to obtain interesting if not authentic results, so the effect at Combermere was hardly new, even if unintentional.

The Chase Vault

A detour, but another interesting occult event had previously occurred to Lord Combermere: in July 1819, Sir

Ashley Hall, Cheshire

The Cage, Lyme Park

Stapleton Cotton, had, as Governor of Barbados, taken part in the opening of the Chase Vault family tomb in Christ Church - the Chases were a local white family with a bad reputation as violent slave-owners, and there was also said to be a least one suicide interred in the tomb.

The circumstances of the 1819 opening were that, on the occasion of a number of burials, the family coffins - made of lead - had been found disturbed, with no traces of entry to the Vault. The vault was resealed by the Governor with his personal seal, but the disturbances continued until the Vault was left empty, and the coffins buried elsewhere. The events attracted a number of commentators, including latterly Arthur Conan Doyle, a staunch spiritualist, who thought 'unused surplus energy' to blame.

LYME PARK

In Lyme Park near Disley in Cheshire a phantom funeral procession with pall bearers and coffin is sometimes said to have seen proceeding towards a small conical hill planted with firs, known as Knight's Low ('low' is another word for a hill or burial mound). Sometimes this is signalled by a distant muffled sound. Here is said to lie Sir Piers (also called Percy or Peter) Legh, who fought at Agincourt (22nd October, 1415) and who died at Paris on 16th June, 1422 of wounds received in the wars in France - according to one version in battle at Meaux while accompanying Henry V. The cortege is followed by a lady in white - not Piers' wife Joan, but a paramour, called perhaps too neatly for a French Lady in white, Blanche - though a ballad of 1867 has 'Agnes'. This must all be rather too much for Sir Piers: according to Earwaker in his History of East Cheshire, he is buried in Macclesfield Church, a fact attested by his epitaph there.

Blanche herself is the subject of separate appearances: she is said to have died of grief, and her body was found near the River Bollin at a spot now called Lady's Grave (not listed however by Dodgson in his definitive Place-names of Cheshire, and not likely on linguistic grounds which should perhaps give the form 'Lady Grave'). She is also said to be the white lady who walks in the house itself.

The source of this story seems to be an account by John Leigh's of 1861 in 'Sir Percy Legh: a legend of Lyme and other ballads'. John Leigh claims to have heard the basis of the story from Thomas Legh at Lyme (1793-1857), with 'adjuncts' from Mrs Legh. His account has Piers dying at Agincourt - probably incorrectly.

The house does indeed have a room called the Ghost Room off the Long Gallery, but this is not claimed to be haunted. Rather, the name arose after a skeleton was discovered in a small secret chamber under the floor - the room is supposed to have a passage leading out to the park, ending at The Cage - a vast folly on a hill. The Cage stands on high ground to the north east of the house and was built by 1737 to replace an earlier sixteenth century building on the site.

It is also interesting to note that the exhaustive history 'The House of Lyme' by The Lady Newton (1917) - some 400 pages and heavily illustrated, makes not a single mention of any ghost. The White Lady has made a number of appearances in recent years, recently coming out of a telephone box.

ASHLEY HALL, CHESHIRE: THE PASSAGE ROOM

Ingham (1886) cites a rather overworked and definitely secondhand piece from The Invisible World concerning Ashley Hall in Cheshire near to Bowden and standing near the River Bollin - it remains a private house. It seems that a houseguest, at some unspecified point in time, was placed in an overflow room called the Cedar Room which had once been a corridor or passage room,. On two successive nights the guest was disturbed by a servant, or some other person, passing through the room at about two in the morning.

The visitor was a melancholy black-eyed lady in white drapery. The houseguest became alarmed because the visitant managed to pass through a door, which on inspection in the morning proved to have been locked. The guest made her excuses and was about to depart on the third day when her hostess confessed all.

This room had in fact previously served as a nursery - much against the advice of the housekeeper who evidently knew its evil repute. The Mistress of the house was only alerted when her small child was found hiding its toys so that the White Lady wouldn't get them.

A CHESHIRE DARK LADY:

'So many devils go in shapes of men....' Anne Fitton.

Mary Fitton was born at Gawsworth, and baptised there on 24th June 1578. In about 1595, when 17 or so, she became a Maid of Honour at Court to Queen Elizabeth. As was usual, she was placed under the tutelage of the Comptroller of the Queen's Household, at that time Sir William Knollys, who was aged 50 and a personal friend of Mary's father.

A portrait of Mary survives showing her in full court dress - low cut across her small breasts on which fall beads and a large pearl; she is wasp-waisted, and wears fashionably elaborate padded arms and a lacy 'standing ruff.' Her hair is adorned with a delicate pearl tiara, and is drawn back in a widow's peak. The lips are full, the overall facial expression

Gawsworth Hall, Macclesfield, Cheshire

slightly petulant. There is a slight venereal strabismus in the eyes, which are not unattractive, though piercing and looking directly at the beholder. The fingers are long, elegant and pale, and bear no rings. Look well: this is Mary at the height of her powers. After this she will not prosper.

Knollys, already married to an older heiress, immediately fell in love with Mary. His letter to her father is unambiguous 'I will with my counsel advise your fair daughter, with my true affection love her, and with my sword defend her if need be. Her innocency will deserve it....'

Mary Fitton was at most a minor player in the tangled web of late Elizabethan politics, as courtiers jostled for positions once the inevitable succession struggle arose. She is noted in 1600 when the Queen attended the marriage celebrations of another maid of honour, at which Mary Fitton led the dances as 'Affection' - 'Affection is false' retorted the Queen.

By that time, Mary was already the mistress of William Herbert, later to become Earl of Pembroke. In February 1601Herbert was sent to prison for this liaison - either the Fleet (which had a foul reputation) or the Tower (slightly better), and Mary, pregnant, was banished from the Court. Herbert refused to marry her. The child died soon after its birth, and Mary was brought home in disgrace only slowly to Cheshire, being too weak to travel. She later went to live with her sister (Anne) in Warwickshire.

It was suggested by Ormerod, the historian of Cheshire on the evidence of Sir Peter Leycester (of Tabley) that Mary subsequently had two more children out of wedlock by a friend of her sister, Sir Richard Leveson. Her mother in Cheshire took this new shame bitterly.

In a letter to her sister Anne she writes:

'I take no joy to hear of your sister and that boy. If it had pleased God when I did bear her [Mary], that she and I had been buried, it had saved me from a great deal of sorrow and grief, and her from shame and such shame as never had Cheshire woman, worse now than ever. Write no more to me of her.'

In any case, by 1607 Mary was finally was married, and had two more children. In 1610 her husband died and she married again. She was again widowed in 1635, and lived on until 1647 when she was aged 69.

But in death the family is reunited and reconciled: in Gawsworth Church there is a painted monument of the Fittons, in which Anne and Mary are represented kneeling behind their mother and father. Reconciled, but not allowed to rest. Something is said to walk the avenue, appearing only to men. She walks on their left hand side. It is perhaps unfortunate that the only recent sighting describes someone obviously not in Elizabethan costume, with their hair loose. Obviously the Fitton connection is to good to lose.

TURBULENT PRIESTS

WARDLEY HALL, WORSLEY: A SCREAMING SKULL

Wardley Hall was built in the short reign of Edward VI (1547-1553) and owned by the family of Tyldesley. It passed to the Downes family in the 1640s. It has one strange possession - a skull in a wall niche. Claims as to the original owner of this skull have swung from a hell-rake under Charles II, to a Catholic martyr.

The Skull in question has been kept in a niche high in the wall of the Great Hall. The niche runs through the wall, and on the far side is a staircase, where the Skull confronts the passer-by at eye level. The apertures are glazed on both sides (but have not always been thus), and oak doors can also be closed to screen the Skull completely from sight. In the past it was believed that the Skull became unhappy if it was closed up - not the case now.

It was believed for many years that the Skull was that of Roger Downes. Despite his family being Catholic, he had been brought up as Protestant because of the death of all near relatives. He is said to have been one of the more profligate members of the notably dissolute court of Charles II, and during a drunken orgy swore that he would kill the first man he met. Rushing "hot from the stews" - presumably the haunts of ill repute in Southwark on the south side of the Thames - he drew his sword on a tailor and killed him. He was acquitted because of his influence at court.

Soon thereafter he was in another brawl on Old London Bridge occasioned apparently by a group of his friends tossing a fiddler in a blanket because he refused to play for them. This time Downes attempted to kill a watchman with his rapier. The watchman parried with his billhook, and severed Downes' head. The body was sent over the side of the bridge into the

Thames, but the head was put into a box, and sent in rather macabre fashion back to his sister at Wardley Hall.

The Skull seems to have disappeared between the mid 1600s and about 1745. At that time the tenant farmer, one Moreton, had been reduced to poverty by the depredations of the Jacobite Army of Bonnie Prince Charlie as it retreated North. In an effort to retrieve his fortune, Moreton was removing walls to set up looms in the Hall, when he uncovered a wooden box. It contained the offending Skull - with all its teeth, and locks of auburn hair.

The Skull was however eventually flung into the moat; a powerful and violent storm followed. Matthew Moreton, the younger brother, convinced that the storm was supernatural, drained the moat and reinstated the Skull.

The Skull was seen again in the late 1790s by a Manchester antiquary, Thomas Barritt. By this time (i.e. within 50 years of its rediscovery), it had acquired a complete folklore: 'if removed, or ill-used, some uncommon noise or disturbance always follows, to the terror of the whole house.' But contrary to more recent practice, the niche was then never glazed or closed with a door: - 'to oblige the skull, which they say is unruly, and is disturbed at the hole not being always open.'

The Skull was also seen by the antiquary Fletcher Moss in the 1890s. In his Pilgrimages to Old Homes, he restates the general belief, adding details: 'Windows were blown in, cattle pined in the stall, and the things were bewitched....there is plenty of testimony to the ill luck that has happened when the skull has been disturbed.

All this made a good tale: except that when the coffin of Roger Downes was finally opened in the family vaults in Wigan Church in 1779, the body was intact, except for a the upper part of the skull being sawn off above the eyes -

Manchester Collegiate Church in 1837

probably by way of post mortem examination to discover why he had died young.

Despite this, the Skull had a stream of visitors, often guided in the Victorian era by the Countess of Ellesmere, who as wife of the Landowner, had a key to the cupboard in which the Skull held court.

Attribution of the Skull to Downes was always dubious. The truth of the matter seems to be better documented, and even stranger and more gory than the story of Roger Downes and his fatal encounter with a London watchman's billhook. The Skull is in all likelihood that of Edward Barlow, born 1585, the son of Sir Alexander Barlow of nearby Barlow Hall who, as a Catholic priest ordained in 1617 took the religious name of Father Ambrose. In the way of all the landed gentry, he was related to the Downes, and on his mother's side to the Breretons.

He had said Mass for many years in hidden chapels at Wardley Hall and Morley Hall, but was at length arrested in 1641 when celebrating Mass at Morley Hall on Easter Sunday 25th April. There had been a parliamentary edict banishing all priests on pain of death by 7th April, which, in order to allow his flock to fulfil their Easter duties, he was then contravening.

He was tried at Lancaster Assizes. The sentence, as was usual, was to be hanged (victims were often cut down alive) then dismembered, quartered, and boiled in tar. This extreme penalty was to serve 'as a terror to the Catholics who were numerous in that county.' He was executed on 10th September, 1641, at the age of 54. His head and quarters were impaled at Lancaster Castle and on the tower of the Collegiate Church at Manchester; the head was rescued by Francis Downes, and hidden in Wardley Hall. Father Ambrose is affirmed to have had light chestnut hair. His life was written by his brother, Rudeskind Barlow, a monk at Douai. There are apparently two portraits of him in existence.

The Catholic version of the story is covered in detail in Dom Bede Camm's 1910 Forgotten Shrines. Roger Downes receives only apologetic mention at the end. In 1930 Wardley Hall became the official residence of the Catholic Bishop of Salford and the skull is now enshrined in a niche on the main staircase. The jawbone has been given to the parish of St. Ambrose, Chorlton where it is now venerated - dispelling yet another myth that the skull could not be moved. In October 1970 Pope Paul VI canonised the forty Martyrs of England and Wales; Ambrose Barlow thereby became an official saint. There are numerous Catholic schools dedicated to Ambrose Barlow in the Manchester area, including Didsbury, where Barlow had been baptised at the Parish Church in 1585.

So which version is true? It is intriguing that the two main claimants to the Skull were diametrically opposed: Libertine and Murderer, versus Martyr and Saint. Or was the Downes tale a cover for the Catholic veneration of a relic ?

THE GORY HEAD OF MOWBRECK HALL

There is another Catholic martyr's skull, now at Lane End House, Mawdesly in Lancashire: again the identity is unclear - possibly that of George Haydock, a Catholic priest and Lancastrian, executed at Tyburn in February 1583 aged twenty eight. The Haydock family was noted for the fact that the father, Evan or Vivian, after the death of his wife, together with his two sons, Richard and George, all became Catholic priests. There was a family tradition of conservatism - another relative, a Cistercian monk - had been hanged for protesting at the suppression of the Northern Monasteries by Henry Tudor, in the reprisals after the Pilgrimage of Grace in 1536.

The Haydock papers published in London in 1888 record the

family tradition of the Gory Head. On the Halloween preceding the arrest of his son George [presumably 31 October 1582] Vivian Haydock stood robed in his vestments at the foot of the altar in the domestic chapel at Mowbreck [his dead wife's former home] awaiting the clock to strike twelve.

As the bell tolled the hour of midnight the "fugitive" beheld the decapitated head of his favourite son slowly rising above the altar whose blood stained lips seemed to repeat those memorable words - the Haydock motto -

> *'Tristitia vestra vertetur in gaudium.'*
> Your sorrow shall be turned into joy.

The father collapses in shock, and is carried to his room. Children arrive to ask for the customary 'somas [soul mass] cakes, with the greeting 'Pray God be merciful for the suffering souls in Purgatory' adding 'Pray for the soul of George Haydock.'

This story looks as though it has been much worked over - the detail is convincing, but the timing is all out. George was alive, according to the historical record, for 15 months after his arrest (November 1581?). The vision can only have been a warning of impending execution. Furthermore the Latin tag is too pat: does it mean that the sorrow of the father at his seeing his son die, will be turned to joy at the thought of his obtaining the crown of martyrdom? Or is it a coded Catholic political message - the sadness of Catholics will be turned to joy by the overthrow of Elizabeth? The same message may be concealed in the famous Tallis' motet 'Spem in Alium' - My Hope lies in none other....' sometimes taken to refer to the hope that Mary Stuart or Phillip of Spain would depose Elizabeth.

Whatever the truth, plainly the Elizabethan period, with its sentencing policy of dismemberment after hanging, followed by public exposure of the parts on pikes, was able to generate a supply of skulls which met the Catholic desire for relics. The natural secrecy of those professing the Old Faith then demanded that these relics be hidden from the sight of non-believers. The accretion of a good folk tale diverted attention from the true nature of the relic, and allowed Catholics a fine mental reservation in talking of the fictitious history of the skull to those who might use information for entrapment. The lapse of time would achieve the rest of the mystery.

AN AMERICAN AT SMITHILLS
Nathaniel Hawthorne and the bloody footprints

In this ghost story the hero is not a Catholic Priest, but a Protestant cleric called George Marsh. His martyrdom is covered in detail in Fox's Book of Martyrs, and more romantically by Roby in his Traditions of Lancashire. These events took place in 1555, during the reign of Mary Tudor - who bears the unfortunate soubriquet of Bloody Mary. But nothing stands still - Roby knew the place as 'Smethhells.' We have retained the modern spelling.

Marsh was summoned to Smithills Hall, and examined by Sir Roger Barton in the Green Chamber concerning his religious views. He refused to abjure his Protestantism, and to adhere to the Catholic Faith (the sticking point was transubstantiation). He is said to have sworn "Between them and me, let God witness - if my cause be just, let the prayer of thine unworthy servant be heard." He then stamped his foot on the flagstone of the floor.

His end was not long in coming: in 1555 Marsh, a 40-year-old widower with children, was sent to Chester. There, in the Lady Chapel of the Cathedral, which was then used as the Consistory Court of the Diocese, he was charged with having "preached and openly published most heretically and blasphemously..... directly against Pope's authority and the

Smithhill's Hall, Bolton, Lancashire

Catholic Church of Rome." He was condemned to death and led through the streets of Chester. There, on nearby Gallows Hill, he was burned at the stake on April 24th. He was buried in St Giles' Cemetery or, as the Official History of Chester puts it, "in it are deposited such of the ashes of the martyr, George Marsh, as could be collected". His martyrdom was the subject of illustrations, which may have fixed the subsequent events in the popular unlettered imagination.

For a cavity remains in the flagstone where he stamped, and is said once a year to become wet and red, as though with blood. As with the screaming skulls, the removal of this flagstone by two boys was followed by terrifying noises, until its safe reinstatement. Marsh himself is said to walk the Hall: in 1732 a figure clad in white vestments was seen in the Green Chamber (according to Roby) or more recently 'glides between the corridors and court room'. It would however be a wise or rash historian of ecclesiastical fashion who could determine with any accuracy the correct protestant clergy vestments in this period of upheaval, when even the surplice might be seen as too 'Roman.'

The story has literary sequellae: the American author Nathaniel Hawthorne (who wrote The Scarlet Letter) was US consul at Liverpool in the 1850s and took the opportunity to familiarise himself with the legends of the surrounding area. He noted in particular the curious story of the Smithills bloody footprint, and incorporated it into not one, but three of his tales. The Ancestral Footstep - an ancient and accursed line whose members left footprints of blood as they walked; the same theme appears in both Septimus Felton (with a 'Sir Forrester') and Dr. Grimshawe's Secret.

The Ancestral Footstep survives only in note form. It leans heavily towards an Edgar Allen Poe Gothic view of the past: the old Lord of Smithills is obsessed with the idea that he could live forever if only a human life is sacrificed for him every thirty years. He chooses as his victim his young and beautiful ward, an orphan girl, and murders her in the woods. But thereafter he leaves a trail of bloody footprints wherever he goes. Unlike other literary creations, this version does not seem to have entered into popular circulation - at least not in Britain.

DICKIE - AN UNADOPTED SCREAMING SKULL

It is noteworthy that there is, or was, another screaming skull at a Tunstead Farm in Derbyshire, near to Disley. It was claimed to be that of a girl murdered there, with a gap to show where the fatal wound had been received. (Another variant makes it a man called Dickie.) So far neither Catholic nor Protestant have laid claim to it.

The Skull was reputed to have a long and varied influence on events, including the collapse of tunnels at Buxton and a landslip in the valley of the River Goyt which diverted the laying of the new London and North West Railway line away from the farm. The Skull also announced by weird and deafening noises either deaths or crises in the family, and took exception to strangers at the farm - even if they were only newly- hired labourers. The Skull had the enviable reputation, on the occasion of it being stolen, of raising a storm of howls not only at Tunstead Farm, but also at Disley, whence it had been taken.

It is interesting to note what most commentators omit, the fact that there are vestiges of a small circle on the hillside above Tunstead, possibly a tumulus from which the Skull came to the farm below. Supporting this is the perforation of the Skull - possibly an iron age trepanning. When the Skull was examined by an eminent Victorian surgeon, he was of opinion that it was the Skull of a female about eighteen years of age, with a small circular hole in the vault of the Skull.

The local name, "Dickie," was apparently only applied to it about the middle of the 1800s when an " address " to it was published in a local newspaper, reprinted in The Ballads and Songs of Derbyshire (1867). When Hutchinson, the author of A Tour Through the High Peak, saw it about the year 1790 he was told by the tenant, Adam Fox, that it had been in the house for "near two centuries," and he records various extraordinary happenings alleged to be connected with it. By the 1900s these appear to have petered out.

THE CIVIL WAR
1642-1647

WYTHENSHAWE HALL

Wythenshawe Hall is a fine example of the black and white Cheshire Hall.. The original Hall was built around 1540 by Robert Tatton, possibly on the site of an earlier medieval building. It was owned by fourteen generations of the Tatton family until 1926, when the estate was sold to provide new housing for the people of Manchester. The Hall and parkland became an art gallery and public park and have been open to the public ever since.

During the Civil War it was owned by Robbert Tatton. Tatton was Royalist, despite being married into the Republican Brereton family. He endured a siege of some 18 months at Wythenshawe with the help of local gentry, servants and soldiers. Tatton was a man of some substance - he was valued at £1,649-2s-8d in 1643. By Sunday 25th February 1644 it was however all over. The Parliamentarians, under a Colonel Duckinfield, were tired of skirmishing and had sent for two pieces of artillery from Manchester. These soon brought Tatton to surrender - but not before a curious incident. One of the serving maids seized a musket, and discharged it a Captain Adams who was astride the walls. Adams fell down dead.

Robert Tatton was dispossessed of the Hall, but not before an inventory was taken, revealing a strange mixture of arms of which a sample is:

'32 Muskeets with Bandoliers and Rests
Foure Large Fowling Pieces
Eight Long Bowes and two Quivers of Arrows, five dozen
A hundred weight of Powder with Matche and Bullets answerable.'

In the 1700s some six bodies were in fact found buried together in the gardens, and it was assumed that these were the casualties of those bitter times. Whatever the true story, someone is said to walk at Wythenshawe - perhaps the maid, perhaps Adams. In good company - facing the Hall is one of those rarities, a statue of Oliver Cromwell, removed to Wythenshawe from its old post next to the Cathedral in Manchester. The statue stood there from 1875 to 1980, when it was moved for urban redevelopment.

THE RING O' BELLS, MIDDLETON: THE SAD CAVALIER

I am indebted to Daniel Parkinson for the following well-told and well-researched stories, taken from his website, *www.mysteriousbritain.co.uk*

The Ring o' Bells is said to be one of the oldest buildings in Middleton, and may be one of the most haunted. Historically the pubs foundations are thought to date back to Saxon times, though legend has it that a druidical temple stood at this spot in the Iron Age - perhaps as a place of ancient sacrifice. In the middle ages it served as a refectory for monks brewing their potent ale, probably in the area where the pubs cellars are currently situated.

The Haunting

The pub is said to be haunted by a Sad Cavalier, who has been nicknamed Edward. The landlord has described how the ghost, dressed in his royalist finery, had been seen on a few occasions, within the pub, and outside by other landlords and a local lady. He also explained that 'Edward' manifested in other less visual ways, including footsteps sounding on the stairs, and other strange noises. He was also known to lay a heavy hand on customers, much to their surprise when they

Wythenshawe Hall, Greater Manchester

turn to find there is no-one in the vicinity.

One of the more frightening incidents was recorded in the Oldham Evening Chronicle of August 18th 1972: the Landlord at that time, Mr George Barnett, was checking barrels in the cellar around midnight when a stone was thrown at his shoulder. He looked around, but ther was no-one in the room. This was the first time that Mr Barnett had been really shaken by a strange event in the pub; he had felt a strange presence, and had even seen a glass slide along the bar but the stone throwing seemed a more aggressive action. He thought someone had perhaps upset the spirit.

The Legend

The traditional story about the Sad Cavalier suggests he was the son of a Lord Stannycliffe of Stannycliffe Hall in the 1600's. The Lord and his family were unwavering Royalists during turbulent times of the Civil War. Unfortunately for them Middleton became more staunchly Parliamentarian, with the Old Boar's Head becoming the Roundhead's headquarters in the area. The story goes that a pocket of Royalist resistance - including the Lord's son - survived in the area, and used the cellars of the Ring o' Bells as a clandestine meeting place. The cellars were linked to Middleton Parish Church by a secret tunnel, by which they could escape if their furtive council was compromised (this passage is said to have been verified by openings which were bricked up within the cellar).

One day somebody betrayed the son of Lord Stanycliffe to the Roundheads whilst he was still in the pub. He managed to flee to the cellars and down the dark tunnel, only to be cut to pieces by Roundheads who were waiting at the church by the passage exit. His body is supposed to have been buried under the flagstones of the cellar, where he is said to remain to this day. Some time in the past helmets and pikes have been discovered under the cellar floor, which date to the 1600s, but no human remains have been found.

At one time the snug (a small room in many old pubs; now often disappearing with modern alterations), which is situated directly over the cellar, was said to have been the room in which the Cavaliers plotted against the might of Cromwell's Model Army.

This served as a focus for the haunting, and a seat within the snug was for long known as the Cavaliers seat, which was always said to be much colder than the rest of the room. Some enthusiasts, who were allowed to spend a night there, recorded colder readings in this area than in any part of the room. While their could be a rational explanation for all of the phenomena that happened in the pub, the wealth of traditions attached to the pub make it one of the more interesting buildings in Middleton.

MARPLE HALL:

Marple Hall, Cheshire is sometimes said to be haunted by the ghost of the daughter of Henry Bradshaw, a previous owner during the Civil War. This must be rather confusing for ghost and any visitor, as the Hall was demolished in 1957.

The Bradshaw family were staunch Roundheads - Henry's brother John was President of the tribunal that condemned to death Charles I. The story is that Henry's daughter had the misfortune to fall in love with a Royalist. He is said to have ill-advisedly visited the Hall while carrying despatches for King Charles I. An old family servant managed by cut through his saddle girths, and he was drowned as he was fording the River Goyt - perhaps much more extensive then. Bradshaw's daughter pined away and eventually died of a broken heart, returning as a spectre to haunt the hall and the banks of the

River Goyt, where her lover was murdered.

'And from the terrace of this ancient hall
The weird-like music trembles through the air
Sad and mournful yet divinely soft
As of a spirit in its last despair'

Old ballads are of course another source of literary invention - this format is not now appreciated, but in its time was probably an effective way of propagating the myth.

Charles I himself is said to have appeared headless at Marple Hall. This seems unlikely, as his grievance over his execution was with the brother John, not Henry Bradshaw. In any case Charles II had his revenge for his father: at his Restoration, John Bradshaw's body was exhumed from Westminster Abbey, and, along with the remains of Oliver Cromwell, dismembered, and hung on the common gallows at Tyburn, their heads being displayed on Westminster Abbey.

Marple Hall still appears on a number of ghostly websites as though it existed. However, it was effectively abandoned by its last owners, the Isherwood brothers, Christopher and Richard, from the 1940s onwards, and allowed to slide into ruin, assisted by vandalism. All that remains is the lintel stone originally set up by Henry Bradshawe in 1658 at the end of the Commonwealth 'and now looking uncannily like a gravestone'. On a visit to the grassed over site of the Hall in the sixties Christopher Isherwood is reported to have "felt no grimness or sadness" at seeing only grass where the house had stood "only wonderfully joyful".

A full and elegiac text with a pictorial record can be found at: http://marple-uk.co.uk/Hall1.htm. It contains tours of the Hall from both 1880 and 1930, neither of which make any mention of the Cavalier or his lover........

PERSISTENT GHOSTS

HANNAH BESWICK: THE GREY LADY OF BIRCHEN BOWER
1758-1981

I am indebted to Daniel Parkinson for this webtale about a Grey Lady, which I have taken from his website and only slightly amended. It is based around a large manor house (now demolished) called Birchen Bower in Holinwood in Oldham, which was famous for its alleged haunting by a Grey Lady called Hannah Beswick:

The Tale

The ghost of Madam Hannah Beswick is still thought to be regular visitor to the industrial estate in New Avenue, which stands on the site of what was once Birchen Bower. She was buried at Harpurhey Cemetery, Manchester, on 22nd July, 1868, but had actually died in 1758, some 110 years before.

In 1745 Prince Charles Edward Stuart, the Young Pretender, marched south towards Manchester with his Highlanders. In common with many citizens and farmers, Hannah Beswick, the Lady of Birchen Bower Manor, though it prudent to bury her money. This view may have been reinforced by the alleged fact that one of her brothers was a supporter of Bonnie Prince Charlie and a captain in his forces.

Shortly after the Scottish invasion had been repelled, John Beswick, one of Hannah's brothers, died - or appeared to do so. He had actually been placed in his coffin and it was only just before the lid was to be screwed down that it was noticed that his eyelids were flickering. A check by Doctor Charles White showed that the man was still alive. He was taken from his coffin and woke from his coma a few days later, to live on for many more years, after having narrowly escaped his premature burial.

This event made such an impression on Hannah Beswick's mind that she immediately made out her will, leaving the whole of her estate to Doctor Charles White on the condition that he and his descendants were to receive the income from the Birchen Bower estates as long as her body was not buried, but embalmed and kept above ground. Every twenty one years the body was to be taken back to Birchen House and left in the Granary for twenty four hours - (or according to some sources for one whole week).

Shortly before her death, the old lady told her relatives that if they were to carry her to the house so that she could die there, she would show them the location of the hidden gold. However, before this could be done, her condition deteriorated and she could not be moved. She died a few days later.

Doctor White had her body embalmed in tar and swathed it in heavy bandages, leaving the face uncovered. The corpse was then placed in a glass-fronted coffin and was kept at Doctor White's house before being moved, on his retirement, to Sale Priory, and then, on his death, to the Museum of the Manchester Natural History Society in Peter Street, Manchester.

Hannah Beswick was on public display in Peter Street from about 1828 until the dissolution of the Society in 1868. The Society was in the process of becoming the present Manchester Museum, attached to the University (then called Owen's College).

Minutes of the Society show that the relatives at the time expressed through their solicitor that they did not wish to be responsible for the disposal of her remains. This seems unkind - the relatives had been allowed the privilege of free entry to the Museum to visit her if they wished during the time of her residence there. After application by the Society's Council to the Home Secretary and with the permission of the Bishop of

Manchester, Hannah Beswick was buried in common ground in Harpurhey Cemetery in an unmarked grave on 22 July 1868.

In the meantime, until his own death, Doctor White is said to have lived in comfort from the rents collected from the Birchen Bower estate.

It was said to be a condition of Hannah Beswick's will that her body should be taken back to Birchen Bower for a period variously said to be one week or one day, every 21 years. True to the condition, the body was laid to rest for the specified period in the old barn. However, during the times that her body lay in the barn, strange things happened on the estate. Horses and cattle, that had been secured in their stables and paddocks overnight, were found loose in the fields the following morning. On one occasion a cow was actually found in the hayloft.

The strange occurrences were not limited to the times when Miss Beswick's body was brought to the barn. It was only shortly after her death, and the house had been divided into several dwellings for the poor, that her ghost was seen in the house.

Her visits became that frequent that the residents who saw her were in no way alarmed. The phenomena always started with the rustling of silk and were followed shortly afterwards by the apparition of the figure of a lady in black, who would glide through the room towards the parlour, where she would disappear at one particular flagstone. In another dwelling, the tenant had a treadle-lathe, which he used for small joinery jobs to earn more money doing work for his neighbours. On several occasions he found what appeared to be an invisible person working away at the lathe as he went in to the workroom.

Joe the Tamer (or of Tamers) moved into the house with his very large family. Joe, who was a handloomer, was extremely poor but his luck seemed to change when he moved into Birchen Bower, because his family were seen to eat well and wear expensive clothes, and they lived in prosperity. This happened whilst his neighbours were starving and caused a great deal of comment and jealousy. It was not for many years that he was to admit that he had discovered a hidden hoard of gold wedges under the floor, whilst digging a treadle-hole so that he could fit a loom in the parlour, at the very spot where Hannah Beswick was seen so many times to disappear. Joe had sold the wedges to a gold dealer in St Ann's Square Manchester, called Oliphants for £3/10s/- each, at a time when a labourer was lucky to earn £1 in a week.

Apparently the visits of Hannah Beswick became more virulent after her hoard had been unearthed - streams of blue light flashed from her eyes, and she radiated anger and menace. Her headless figure was also seen near to a pond, and strange noises emanated from the barn.

In the early part of the 20th century, Hannah was also seen standing beside an old well, and has been seen visiting the site of the old barn in quite recent times. Perhaps she had hidden part of her hoard there. Madam Beswick is still said to haunt the area of the site on which Birchen Bower once stood. In April, 1956, several night-shift workers saw her shadowy figure at the Ferranti Works. Over a period of a few days she was seen by more than 40 people. She was also seen standing at the works' entrance in 1968. In 1972, she was seen wandering through the works' canteen. There was another reported sighting in 1981.

Now this is a gripping tale - Hannah Beswick dying in 1758,but still causing problems in the 1980s; but very little seems to be verifiable.

Dr Charles White was indeed an eminent physician/surgeon who at the time of Hannah Beswick's death owned a house called Cheetwood Hall near the foot of Cheetham Hill in Manchester. It was at the latter house that Miss Beswick died, which White may have used as a nursing home. It is thought that Dr White embalmed her at his own home at another address in Manchester. Miss Beswick was for some years a patient of Dr White and had a fear of being buried alive.

Post mortem, she was said to have been kept as a mummy for some years at Ancoats Hall. She was later transferred to the roof of "The Priory" at Sale, Cheshire in a lead-lined coffin and where Dr White lived latterly until his death in 1813. There is a record of the coffin in which she was kept being burned around 1890 by the old gardener who had worked on the estate for the previous 40 years.

The mummy was bequeathed by Dr White to a Dr. Ollier and left eventually by Ollier in his will to the Manchester Natural History Society. Thus Hannah Beswick arrived at their Museum in 1828.

The stories around Hannah Beswick at least have three threads, which will probably never now be disentangled, and may have been spun by interested parties in the past:

That she lived in Birchen Bower, and buried her money there. She arranged to be mummified to prevent her brother, whom she disliked, from getting the inheritance.

That Dr White owed her a lot of money to be paid with interest after her burial and that he evaded payment by embalming the body and keeping it above ground.

That she had a relative who had nearly been buried alive, so she had a great fear of the same thing happening to her. By the terms of her will, Dr White was authorised to embalm her. In return for guarding her from interment and checking annually together with two reliable witnesses that she was still in her coffin, she left him the "Priory" estate in Sale, Cheshire.

Other rumours around the time of her death denied that she ever requested this course of unorthodox disposal of her mortal remains in that she had bequeathed £400 towards funeral expenses. The residue of which, Dr White being the executor of her will, was supposed to give to the relatives but that by embalming her body he was enabled to avoid this issue and appropriate the funds for himself.

The terms of Hannah Beswick's will of 25th July 1757 are not secret: they were examined at Chester in the 1900s (see Manchester Notes and Queries, 1904, Query No. 10,356). There is no mention of embalming in the will, nor that the body be returned to Birchen Bower; Dr White was to receive only £100; and £400 was left to defray funeral expenses. Indeed extracts from the will show a grasp of detail which suggests an old lady in control of her faculties, rather than the eccentric malevolent witch who is usually portrayed. There is however another article from the Manchester News of 1866 which states that the property bequeathed in the will was still in dispute - this included 'her messuage situate in Chadderton known by the name of Birchen Bower.'

A likely series of events is that Hannah Beswick did have a fear of being buried alive, and asked Dr White to keep her above ground until signs of her death were obvious. Embalming was one way to arrange this. But White already had a collection of 'wet and dry' exhibits, and the temptation to add a mummy proved too strong. Against this should be set the fact that White was a man of some probity and reputation.

The focus of Hannah's return was Birchen Bower. The tale of the cow in the hayloft was reported in the Oldham Chronicle of

2nd July 1864 - though by this time it was believed that Hannah had died in the Old House - then 'being pulled down.' So, the motive was revenge for the Old Hall being pulled down.

The Ferranti hauntings are even more interesting. This tale was picked up by the Oldham Evening Chronicle of April 24th 1956, but the 35 or so workers who claimed to have seen something reported a 'black raincoat and a trilby hat.' Not quite the silks or mobcap of the 18th century. There is a written report on the Hannah Beswick affair dated February 2nd 1963 by Harry Harvey, who was employed in the Ferranti factory on nightshifts at the time: 'I cannot say that at any time did I see or hear anything to cause alarm.' Furthermore, Harvey points out that Hannah's brother John cannot have been a Captain in the Young Pretender's forces: he had been dead some 9 years when the Pretender arrived in Manchester. His will also exists and is dated September 10th 1737. There was a John Beswick in the Pretender's forces, but sadly for the tale, not Hannah's brother.

One of the mysteries of Hannah Beswick is that we have a plethora of documents, rumours and sightings, but no pictures of her. Harry Harvey searched, but found only a description by Philip Wentworth, historian of Blackley:

'The body was well preserved but the face was shrivelled and black. The legs and trunks were tightly bound in a strong cloth such as is used for bed ticks [a stiff kind of mattress cover material] and the body, which was that of a little old woman, was in a glass coffin-shaped case.'

Ferranti has now gone too, and the site is occupied by the Mirror Newspaper Group. Hannah Beswick is buried in Harpurhey in an unmarked grave.

GODLEY GREEN: HAUNTED 1830-1880-1906

The Godley Green hauntings in the Hyde area deserve to be better known, simply because of the continuity of activity sustained over a long period. They are first recorded in the 1830s when a poltergeist was observed at an unnamed farm. The activity was typical: doors thrown open, beds rocked and the bedclothes torn off; footfalls on the stairs; firedogs moved about, pans rattled or thrown to the floor; the sound of someone sweeping. It is perhaps significant that the events took place at a time when there was much unemployment locally, and also much hunger.

The Pastor of Hyde Chapel, the Reverend James Brooks, who was resident there for most of his life, was called in to lay what was taken to be a ghost. Brooks was a person of some note: in 1829 he preached a funeral sermon to a crowd of over 6,000 people mourning the so-called "May's Disaster." 200 people, protesting against unemployment had crammed into a local inn, the Norfolk Arms: the theme of the speaker was "It is bread we want and it is bread we must have" when the floor collapsed and 29 died.

Brooks spent several nights in the afflicted rooms of the farm, praying and reading the Bible, after which the malevolent spirit appears to have departed for a time. The spirit did however return, though its visitations were less frequent. In the 1880s the children of the farm are reported to have seen a rocking chair set itself in motion. A passing farm labourer was too frightened to stop it, but the farmer's wife, perhaps with great common sense, stilled it by simply sitting in it.

The explanation given was that an old woman, the last survivor of the previous tenant's family had died in a rocking chair, and her restless ghost wandered the house as though looking for some object.

The farm seems to have attracted psychic attacks: there was also a patch of ground in the garden where nothing would ever grow. In the 1890s human bones were removed from this spot, but it still remained bare.

In 1906 the tenant's wife was returning to the farm from nearby Gee Cross, when the thorn hedge in the lane - of some height - began to rock violently, despite it being a still day. Her fear was heightened both by the fact that her brother was lying sick at the farm, and by the appearance of a woman in white from behind the hedge, who seemed to be leaving the farm. Hurrying home she arrived to find that her brother had just died.

WHALEY BRIDGE:
THE BIRD AND LINEN JACKET 1823 - 1874

This is another tale with a starting point: on July 16th 1823 one William Wood of Eyam was going to Whaley Bridge from Manchester, when he was violently attacked by three men for the cash he was carrying; he was murdered by three sailors, by having his head struck repeatedly with a large stone. He was probably carrying about £100 in cash - two years wages for the average labourer. When his body was found and removed to the nearby Joddrell Arms (now adjacent to Whaley Bridge Railway Station), it was noted that there was a depression in the earth where his head had lain. One of the murderers, Robert Dale was apprehended, and hanged at Chester on 21st April 1824. A second murderer Taylor (aka Bradley) committed suicide in gaol. The third evaded capture but is said to have confessed on his deathbed in 1855.

There is a very full coverage of this crime, the Dale trial and the subsequent haunting in Cheshire Notes and Queries of 1886, taken mainly from the Stockport Advertiser of July 18th and 25th 1823.

As in many tales, it was alleged that no grass would grow on the spot where the battered head had rested, but more peculiarly, that it could not be filled in. The depression was said to be some four inches deep, and sixteen to eighteen inches long. John Fox, who lived nearby in 1859 was said to have often filled it with stones - but to no avail. The stones were always found nearby, and the hollow empty again. On one occasion he described feeling something 'brushing rapidly past him, back and forth, with a sound like the wings of a large bird'. On another occasion he saw a linen jacket 'or singlet' hanging on a wall near to the depression, but it vanished as he tried to reach for it and there was no one on the other side of the wall.

In 1874 a stone memorial was erected near the spot. The tale of the hole was still being attested by local people when Albert Fryer, who wrote Wilmslow Graves visited the area in 1888. He himself found a small walnut sized pebble in the hole, and a friend found two; nonetheless the constant local belief was that nothing would ever grow there. The tale continues to resurface occasionally in books, though it must now be fading into oblivion.

ORPHANS AND STRAYS

THE JOHN RYLANDS LIBRARY, DEANSGATE

The John Rylands Library in Deansgate has the distinction of being called the most beautiful neo-Gothic building in Northern Europe. Its fine red sandstone, now cleaned of Manchester's soot, is off-set by ornate gold inscriptions and black wrought iron gates and lamps. Inside is housed one of the greatest collections of religious books in the country (including the original works of both Wesleys). It was the gift of a rich Manchester merchant, John Rylands, and his wife, Enriqueta Augustina, who made an inspired choice in Basil Champneys, architect of Mansfield College, Oxford. But there are those who say that the site is an old burial ground; others that it was merely a school.....

Inside, the library has the atmosphere of a church - quiet, orderly, with the Fathers of the Reformation gazing down from stone plinths. But the faces of two greenmen gaze unnervingly at you, out of the art-nouveau ironmongery at the top of the main staircase. The silent figure of a lady has been seen in the upper gallery and also in the basement. Footsteps have been heard early in the winter darkness when the library is being made ready, and doors open and shut with a bang. Staff have felt a ghostly hand on their shoulder or tugging at their clothes. The bags of visitors have been seen to swing in motion on their pegs unaided. The slightly brooding presence seems to dissipate if greeted, and on one occasion may have given a warning when an elderly lady fell on the long stone staircase. It was last seen in about 1997.

THE SOUND OF HOOVES: CHELFORD

Somewhere on the A537 from Knutsford to Chelford in the 1800s, a group of three people passed the turnpike at about

The John Rylands Library, Deansgate, Manchester

midnight in a horse-drawn gig. The young man in the centre was noted by the gatekeeper as being supported by the other two. Next day his dead body was found by the road at Ollerton. His clothes and his soft hands suggested someone of some social standing, but his identity was never discovered, though the clothes were retained as evidence for many years.

The story passed into local legend. It occurs in Henry Green's 1869 History of Knutsford. But the sequel is even more astonishing. It occurs in Cheshire Notes and Queries for 1889, when a reader, Albert A Birchenough, wrote in to express his astonishment at the Green story. In October 1872 he had been walking to Chelford, and having passed Norbury Booths, was halfway along his journey. It was a Sunday, the countryside was silent, and the night was clear, with a starry sky. Behind him he heard a 'conveyance' with the rattling of wheels and horses. He moved aside to let it pass, but it seemed to stop some 20 yards behind him. There was a sound of voices and two or three persons jumping down.

He turned, and went back to ask for a lift, but there was nothing there. A passer-by came up from the Chelford direction, and eyed with suspicion someone wandering around in the road at that hour. Birchenough explained the reason ,and asked if there were any turnings here - 'no'.Perhaps they were poachers? 'Hardly likely to be in a gig'.

So, some decades after the events, a stranger notes a strange event; it takes him several decades more to realise the meaning of what he heard....

THE LAST HUNTSMAN:
Hough Hall, Moston, Manchester

Finally, a story from Moston, itself near to Boggart Hole Clough. Hough Hall is an Elizabethan period stone and timber building situated in the township of Moston. The house was reportedly built for Hugh Shacklock, a merchant of this district, from about 1500 to 1525. Moston is now mainly built-up. The following undated tale is from Cheshire Notes and Queries of January 1888, and looks back to a time when Moston was still open countryside - perhaps around 1800 ? It was told at second hand to Charles Roeder, the geologist and folklore collector by the 'devout antiquarian' Thomas Lancashire about one Robert Glossip, who recounted a strange meeting early one morning in the grounds of the Hall, with the ghost of Captain Hough and his hounds:

'When I was a young fellow, I was the carter at Hough Hall, and one morning in the summer time I was asked to come very early, as it was washing day and they had no coal. The nearest coal pits in those days were at Oldham. So I went to the Hall just as the day was beginning to break. I could see the [horses] were in the crofts and went to catch them; both horses stood with their ears pricked, they were looking as if something had startled them.

This caused me to look around, when a short distance away I was horrified to see a Hunter on horseback surrounded by his hounds. I knew at once this was Captain Hough's spirit, surrounded by his shadow hounds.'

Glossip had in fact heard his neighbours say that the Captain and his hounds had often passed them at night in full cry.

THE FAIREEN AT MOSTON

Again at Moston, another tale collected by Roeder in Cheshire Notes and Queries for 1888, this time about fairies. It is charming in that it places the action in a particular field (Buckhold Field, which might still be identifiable today from the 1840s Tithe Maps); it is datable (1830-40) and attributed (to "old Sammy Wharmby"). But like many fairy tales, this goblin gold, so near to Manchester, is not quite what it seems....

'Going across to Moston Hall we come upon the Buckhold field. [this is probably book-hold or registered land]. Here once a ploughman was ploughing in the field and noticed when he got to the headland [where room was left for the plough to turn] two or three little folk standing, one of which held a in his hand a broken back-spittle [a wooden shovel, with a small handle, used for turning oat-cakes], also a little hammer and a few nails.

The Little folk were what were called in Moston "faireen." Upon seeing the ploughman come near to where they stood, they retreated and disappeared, leaving their back-spittle, hammer and nails upon the ground.

The ploughman judged the faireen wished him to repair their back-spittle, and he at once began to do so, leaving it where he found it. He went on with his ploughing. After turning over another furrow, he returned to the place, where he had left the back-spittle, when to his surprise he saw a tankard of good ale awaiting him.'

A tale well told, but almost identical with that told by James Bowker in his Goblin Tales of Lancashire of 1883 about the Fylde District. Alas for oral tradition.

A SALE SÉANCE in 1874

Clara Alcock was the daughter of a Sale clergyman and in the 1870s she kept a journal. She seems to have been about 16 at the time, and working as a teacher. Volume III is in the

Manchester Central Library, running from July 1874 to May 1875. It is a record and commonplace book, with darker undertones of visits to the squalid homes of some of her pupils, deaths of relatives (one from diphtheria), together with this record of a not very serious attempt at table turning in September 1874. Clara was asked to tea by a family friend, Mrs Schott, at which a number of young men were present. There was a very Victorian period of cards, piano and singing, and then:

'After tea our time was curiously spent. I feel as if it was a dream, and I can't make anything of it however much I think of it. But this is what we did. We turned the lamps low: Mrs Will. fetched a gentleman's hat and put it on the middle of an oval table they use for cards. We all sat round it. Mr Edgar Haslam was opposite to me: Mr Robert Heywood was on his left hand, and then Mr Louis Haslam on Mr Edgar's right hand: Mr and Mrs William were sitting on one chair.

We all put our hands on the brim of the hat: I only put one hand on and put the other under it to prevent me from leaning any weight on it. After a few minutes the hat began to jerk about. Mr Edgar said we ought to feel very religious: so Mr Louis said " For what we are about to receive" and then said bits of several hymns altering them to suit the occasion.

Then Mr Edgar inquired "Is there a spirit present?" on which the hat gave three bumps on the table, which meant yes. Then he said: "Will you make a manifestation?" Three more bumps. Then my hands and arms felt a pricking, something like a galvanizing. They asked "Is Miss Alcock a medium?" Three bumps. "Are we all in our right places?" One bump = No. [The company rearranges itself to suit.]

"Can you turn this table?" "Yes" So we took the hat off and put our hands on the table. "Will you make a manifestation?" "Yes" "Knock about a bit"

It began to dance violently and nearly fell over.
"Now keep still again" It did so..........
"What time is it?" on which it tilted on one side and knocked
one foot sharply on the floor ten times.
"Is it time for Miss Alcock to go?" "Yes"
So I came home. I can't make head or tail of it, but that's just
what passed, and those are all the questions I can remember.'

It is interesting to note that by the 1870s the context of table manifestations was already very formalized, and had become another parlour game. There is also a subtle undercurrent of flirtation with the young men, properly chaperoned by the spirit in breaking up the party.

THE LAYING OF GHOSTS

*....Come No More Whilst Holly Is Green
Or Water Down A Ditch Shall Run*

From: The Snydale Ghost, by John Clough, Bolton Journal Office, 1882. Cited by WEA Axon, Lancashire Gleanings.

Northen Churchyard: Laying The Gatley Shouter

Crime is subject to fashion too. The Gatley Shouter was collected by Moss in 1891 with slightly different versions in 1894 and 1898 'as it was told to me by an old man who was then over 80. I am not sure whether he was present at the great hunt, or only remembered it.' This would place the events at least in the 1820s or 1830s.

The Gatley Shouter was a soul condemned to walk for a certain time the night because in life he had retailed watered milk. His name was Jim Barrow, and he has acquired a reputation for great stinginess: 'desperate fond of brass' - hence the milk watering.   In death the Devil - 'Owd Scrat' - had got hold of his soul, and was torturing it steadily over a slow fire. When the moon was full and hell getting too hot, Jim would rise from his grave in Northen Churchyard, and slip into Carr Lane in Gatley, moaning all the while:

*'Milk and Water sold I ever,
Weight and measure gave I never.'*

His repeated presence on Gatley Carrs eventually provoked the local residents to invite Resurrectionists (who had a thriving business selling fresh corpses) to remove Jim's body and hopefully the soul with it - Northenden at this time had a bad reputation for premature resurrection. The Resurrectionists politely refused, and got on with removing fresher corpses for the medical students - for example, in January 1831 the bodies of two recently buried local women were found in a field at Alderley, neatly wrapped in sacks and awaiting collection. The perpetrator received two years imprisonment.

Now Northen Church had recently acquired a new parson, who decided to lay the ghost of Jim Barrow for once and for all. The tale, as told by Moss suddenly moves into the local vernacular, which is repeated here for its quaintness:

'Jim Barrow....cum fro Cross Acres, t'other side o Gatley. Them Gatley folk was allus a gallus [wild] lot. Owd Jim wur desprit fond o brass an e stuck to a' e could lay ode on. E'd a flayed two fleas fur one 'ide, e wud, {skinned two fleas for their hide] and when e deed Owd Scrat got 'im an e warmt 'im, an Jim mi't be eard a neets [nights] moanin "Oh dear, oh dear, wa-a-tered milk, wa-atered milk" till folks got plaguey feart [afraid] a goin yon road arter dark.

Now there come a new passon [parson] to Northen, a scholar fresh from Oxford or Rome or someweers, chok-fu o book-larnin, an e played the hangment wi a th' ghoses i' these parts an e said e'd tackle im.

So e got aw th' parish as could read or pray a bit to cum wi their bible, an one neet [night] when the moon were out Owd Scrat mun a [must have] bin firin up, for th' Shouter wur rarely bein fettled [handled] by th way he moaned

An the folk got round im an they drew toart [towards] one another in a ring like, and kep cumin closer till at last they'd gotten im in a corner i' the churchyard by the yew tree an the Passon was on the grave an e whips a bit o chalk out o 'is pocket an draws a holy ring around them aw an aw the folk joins 'ands, and pray desprit loike, an the Passon ops about an shouts an bangs the book till e's aw o a muck sweat. An 'e prayed at 'im in Latin too, mind yo, as weel as English, an th

poor ghost moans and chunners [mutters] an gets littler and
littler till he fair sweals [melts] away like a sneel [snail or slug]
that's salted. An at last the devil wur drove out of him, an lets
im abide as quiet as a mouse. E's now under yon big stone near
the Passon's gate. Yo may see it for yosen [yourself]. It's theer
now.'

Northenden Church is still there, as is the Parson's gate and
the Old Rectory. The stone is not visible, but may be in the
rectory garden somewhere - now a private house. But there is
another house in the same row: it has a bricked up passage
under the road to the Church, and a presence.....There is
unfortunately a very similar tale told at Burslem in
Staffordshire, with a similar rhyme about watered milk.

HAWTHORNE HALL WILMSLOW: LAYING EPHRAIM ?

Fletcher Moss is at times enigmatically silent about ghosts in
his 1900s six volume work: Pilgrimages in Cheshire and
Shropshire. Of Hawthorne (or Harethorne) Hall at Wilmslow
he has a tale but will only say that had an informant, who
seems to have given him a garbled tale of two brothers called
Birtles at the Hall (other sources cite the name as Ephraim
Ridgway. They found a gold treasure - possibly with the
Devil's assistance. One of them, Ephraim, dies; but:

E'd us't to come again [as a ghost] an men set up aw neet [all
night] to lay him, sayin they'd fettle him [sort him out], an they
dug im up agen, an when the coffin were opent, there e were,
fresh as need be, aw comfortable like, wi' is ed packt up in
common Lindow black turves.'

This weird little tale begs more questions than it answers: a
golden treasure, a body or head coming preserved out of
Lindow - it sounds too much like an echo of a bog corpse like
Lindow Man, with perhaps Celtic gold finery around him.......

LAYING THE SALFORD POLTERGEIST OF 1959:
A TRADITIONAL PURSUIT ?

The Salford Poltergeist appeared in a Tully Street house on Christmas Eve 1959, with manifestations until February 1960. The interesting aspect is that the manifestation took the form of two sets of loud noises - one like blows being struck rhythmically, another like a heavy object bounding along. Neighbours in the same street were reported as hearing them too.

Reports at the time said that both Water and Gas Board officials examined the dwelling, together with scientists from Manchester University. These latter said that some kind of code might be contained in the sounds.

The Reverend Edward Dimond, vicar of St James's Church in Broughton also visited the house to hear the banging. He subsequently said that they were caused by a resentful spirit, trapped on the earth plane. The Bishop of Manchester gave permission for exorcism. The news attracted a large crowd, which had to be dispersed by the police. The service seemed to work, and the troubled spirit was despatched onwards to the afterlife. There was also a suggestion that the focus of the noises was a young boy in the house, with whom the spirit was trying to communicate.

Now this tale looks like a modern orphan and stray: but consider this from Robert Roberts' laconic account of pre First World War Salford 'A Ragged Schooling':

'Besides the poltergeists which came on their own, we had a gentleman who fetched them up. Mr Carley, a gloomy man with a heavy moustache, ran séances as a sideline in one of the parloured houses nearby.........[he] had recently been wakened during the small hours by a frightful crash in their front room, yet not a thing appeared to have been disturbed.'

Clegg Hall, Rochdale

Salford, as the world's first industrial slum, was plainly heavily visited by noisy spirits, proving that antiquity is no pre-qualification. Our modern practice would be to look for a focus - probably a young girl. Mr Carley turned to his familiar, a rather unlikely 'Red Indian' psycho-squatting in Salford - and perhaps more common as spirit guides then. The guide offered a solution during the next séance: the noise was the sound impact of 'spirit vibration' from a tree which had crashed 'hundred of miles away!' Mr Carley's gloom was reinforced: the tree contained the wood which was going to make his coffin. This is a neat, reversed and foreshortened version of the ghostly Northumbrian 'Cauld Lad of Hilton,' - the acorn is not yet fallen from the tree, that's grow to an oak, that's to make the cradle, that's to rock the babe that will grow to a man , that will lay me.

CLEGG HALL: TWO ILLITERATE BOGGARTS LAID

Clegg Hall near Rochdale was haunted by not one, but two Boggarts; these are usually said to be the ghosts of two children murdered for their inheritance while their father was absent at the Crusades. As boggarts they affirmed they would only be laid if presented with a body and soul. Since no-one locally wanted to make the ultimate sacrifice, they were offered instead a cockerel and an old boot - sole in lieu of soul, it being well know that, in contrast to cobblers, parsons can heal souls.

The boggarts do not appear to have been completely stupid, for they agreed to be bound over only until the cock and the sole were consumed. Local tradition had it that the boggarts duly reappeared some time later, after digesting this coq-au-boot meal.

THE SQUIRE OF KEMPNALL AND CLEWORTH

Not quite a ghost story, but interesting in that it prefigures the Lancashire Witch Trials of nearly twenty years later. In 1594 Nicholas Starkie was Squire of Kempnall and Cleworth in Lancashire. Two of his children became possessed - his daughter Anne '...with a certain fearful starting and pulling together of her body' and his son John who was unable to stop shouting. He called in John Hartley, described as a noted conjuror - here in the ancient sense of one who conjures or summons spirits. Hartley's use of 'certain popish charms and herbs' seemed to give temporary relief, and he took up residence at Cleworth - a good billet no doubt. He then made extortionate demands, including a house with grounds and a annual pension - otherwise the possession would return.

John Dee, then Warden of Christchurch Manchester (and himself under constant suspicion of being a wizard) was consulted by Starkie, but he refused to become involved. Dee "utterly refused to meddle with the affair, and advised the father to consult with godlye preachers and appoint a private fast." He sent for Hartley, and "so sharply rebuked him that the children had more ease for three weeks after."

The devils were finally exorcised by a preacher, John Darrell, after the clergy had been locked up for two days with the afflicted. One woman saw 'all the while a dark mist [which] dazzled her eyes....It went out in the likeness of a crow's head, round, and sat in a corner of the parlour with darkness around it for a while. Then it went with a great flash of fire out of the window, that all the parlour seemed on fire to her only.'

It was however, Dee's curate, Matthew Palmer, who undid Hartley. He happened to go in as Hartley was praying over a woman in a fit. He demanded what he was doing.
"`Praying.'
"`Thou pray! thou canst not pray,' quoth I. `What prayer

canst thou say?'

"`None,' saith he, `but the Lord's Prayer.'

"`Say it,' quoth I, the which as I remember, he could not say." In fact 'he began to fumble about it very ill-favouredly, but could not for his life say it to the end.'

Palmer accused him of being a witch, sent him to Lancaster Assizes, where Hartley was hanged for conjuroring evil spirits. Ominously, the rope is said to have broken on his first drop. Darrell himself, the hero of the tale, subsequently got into hot water for apparently inciting 'The Nottingham Boy' William Sommers, to counterfeit possession. The two cases also generated considerable literature, culminating in the 1612 Witch Trials.

All this is good stuff - if it had not been for the fact that Nicholas Starkie's wife was a Catholic, and was never cured of her possession. There was, as usual, a story of a dispute over inheritance (the main pursuit and entertainment of the landed classes of the time).

Darrell was one of the Puritan faction within the Church, and was perhaps using the power to exorcise spirits as a way of furthering the Puritan cause. One final result was the banning of all unlicenced exorcisms in England under Church canons of 1604 - indeed, no more licences were given to conforming members of the Anglican Church in the 17th century.

ALDERLEY: A bird and iron bottle.....

This tale from Alderley is peculiar in several respects. It is a tale of rural infidelity, which is the motivation for a haunting - many ghosts seem to appear for no good reason. It occurs in Cheshire Notes and Queries for March 1881, under the initials TJ - again probably Thomas Jarman of Stockport. Jarman claims here to have grown up in Alderley and imbibed the folklore 'in the chimney corner of an old cottage which yet stands between the Soss Moss and the Beech wood' (sic).

As in many instances the tale must be set somewhere in the 1810-30s. Jarman (if it were he) heard that a few years before he sat in that inglenook as a child, there was a gamekeeper called Firbank, who lived in the area with his wife. Jarman is coy, but Mrs Firbank seems to have fallen in love with another - the "green-eyed monster" made its appearance and 'domestic felicity was ended.' Firbank fell ill, and realising he was dying, he made his wife promise that she would not marry the cause of his jealousy - a promise she did not keep.

Old people declared that following the new marriage, Firbank could not rest in his grave, and began to play tricks on them. As they sat by the fire, a third unwelcome chair would be drawn up to the hearth, and by degrees the outline and then the accusatory figure of Firbank would appear, glaring at the newly-weds, but never speaking a word.

They went to the Rectory (Jarman describes it as the sweetest spot on earth - the Latin inscription over the front door reads 'Deus nobis haec otia fecit' ("God made for us this life of ease"). The rector upbraided them for what seemed to him verification of Firbank's suspicions, but his professional interest was doubtless engaged, and he agreed to lay the ghost.

The Rector visited Henshall, the local blacksmith at his smithy near to the Beech wood, and asked him to make a large cast-iron bottle. In order to avoid being labelled as the "ghost-bottler" ('in country places nicknames were more easily acquired than got rid of') the smith decided to make the bottle at midnight. It was delivered to the house of Firbank (implying that not only was Mrs Firbank sharing her favours but also her former marital bed with her new husband.) The Rector went through the form of words, and the ghost was laid with surprising ease in the bottle which was screwed shut and buried in the churchyard.

But Firbank rose again the following night with hideous noises, to haunt the couple. They fled to the Rector, who realised that the making of the bottle in the dead of night had been an error. Firbank, 'always a shrewd and far-seeing man' knew that the bottle was flawed in some way, and had allowed himself to be laid far too easily. Now he would be more difficult to deal with.

a small bird flitting in the Beech Wood

Henshall made a second bottle of better iron, and this time in the daylight. Firbank realised that more serious preparations were underway, and begged the Rector for some modicum of liberty. After some parleying, he was permitted to appear as a small bird, flitting only a certain distance round a particular tree in the Beech Wood. He was once again secured in an iron bottle, this time buried in the wood, to no more annoy the living.

There is an elegant footnote to all this: the Right Rev. Dr. Edward Stanley was the second son of Sir John-Thomas Stanley. He was born in 1779 and took holy orders in 1805. He was then appointed Rector of Alderley by his father, where he continued for about thirty-two years, until 1837, when he became Bishop of Norwich. He was celebrated as a geologist, botanist, and entomologist ; but his favourite study was ornithology, and his key work was Familiar History of British Birds, their Nature, Habits, and Instincts. How appropriate, if true, that he should wish a ghost into a bird until Judgement Day.

The laying of ghosts was no idle occupation for a parson: Fletcher Moss has this addition to the Alderley Tale; 'A gamekeeper with a black dog used to walk at Authorley, till th' passon laid 'im; but th' passon's yure [hair] wur as black as a crow th' day afore, an in th' morn it wur as grey as a badger; so he mun a bin rarely feart.' [He must have been really afraid]. There is no place I can find called Authorley, though one renowned local source cites it as a form of Alderley
.

The portraits we have of Edward Stanley show him as dark-haired and strikingly handsome: he was himself made of cast iron, and seems to have come in to Alderley as a reforming minister, caring for the sick and the poor, opposing public drunkenness and on one occasion stopping single handed a prize fight -'The whole field was filled, and all the trees round about.....I saw the Rector coming up the road on his little black horse quick as lightning, and I trembled for fear they should harm him. He rode into the field and just looked quick around (as if he thought the same) to see who there was that would be on his side. But it was not needed - he rode into the midst of the crowd, and in one moment it was all over; there was a great calm; the blows stopped; it was as if they would all have wished to cover themselves up in the earth - all from the trees fell down directly - no one said a word, all went away humbled.' (Memoirs of Edward and Catherine Stanley, 1880).

Local research in 2002 produced the following interesting commentary on the Firbank tale:

"In my family oral tradition, the transference of the ghost into a bird was not known, nor were the two bottles. Edward Stanley simply conjured the ghost of Firbank into an iron bottle, made by the blacksmith, and threw it into Radnor Mere [in the present Alderley Park]. The gamekeeper's house still stands, on Hocker Lane. The incident of the iron bottle is so rare in English folklore that I suspect that it was an historical event, perhaps given force by the wider knowledge of folklore and great understanding of Edward Stanley. He would have known the power of the dramatic gesture."

Alan Garner, Personal Communication, October 2002

Richard Brereton cast into a swallow.

The tale of Firbank, the Alderley Gamekeeper, is matched by a similar tale from Worsley, where Richard Brereton, who inherited the Old Hall in 1570, was only partly laid after his death in 1598 by the sacrifice of a cockerel - he had wanted a human sacrifice. The exorcists pursued him onto the local moss, where they persuaded him to appear henceforth in a form less terrifying - a swallow. This form of apparition as a bird has also attached itself to Brereton's wife, Dorothy née Legh, who also walks Worsley Old Hall. C. Elsie Mullineux says in her pamphlet Ghosts, Little Hulton, Walkden, Worsley that her family tradition states clearly the swallow to be Brereton.

a form less terrifying - a swallow

THE AUTHOR'S FAREWELL

How to end a book of ghost stories ?

There is a slight but charming legend from Knutsford, where language and folklore seem to mingle. As befits Knutsford, it concerns nuts (not unfortunately King Canute who may or may not have given his name to the town). An elderly lady was buried in the Old Churchyard at Knutsford, with the unusual stipulation that a small sack of hazel nuts in their shells be placed beneath her head. This was duly done - but the nuts proved uncomfortable, so she turned in her coffin. T'other side was no better, so she arose from her grave one moonlight night, and proceeded to crack and eat the hazel nuts, seated on her own tombstone. She then folded the sack for a pillow, retired to her coffin and troubled the mortal sublunary world no more.

But one nut had rolled away unseen. It sprouted and grew. It fruited and its own nuts attracted the attention of local truants. As Henry Green noted in 1869 in his small, but beautifully written book *Knutsford*: the nut-tree 'was looked upon with wonder, as an undeniable witness for all who love the marvellous and believe in church-yard verities.'

THE DOGS THAT DIDN'T BARK

Well, not quite 'farewell'. The problem with ghosts and ghost stories in Britain is that there are too many of them. Headless, Hairy, White Ladies, Grey Ladies, Monks, Skulls. It is a relief, but also a puzzle to come across a place where the curator says there is nothing to report. Here are a few:

Gorton Monastery

Gorton Monastery, designed by EW Pugin, abandoned by the Franciscans after a final Mass in 1989, and now deconsecrated, desolate and vandalised, does not seem to have attracted any visitants. Yet.

Vale Royal Abbey

The Northwich webguide cites Vale Royal as 'the site of the largest Cistercian Abbey Church in England. Before excavations 1911-1912 this distinction was thought to belong to Fountains Abbey Church. Indeed, until these excavations, not only had the monastery disappeared from view but even its exact site was doubtful. Before 1911 most local people had only a vague notion that a great abbey had once stood at Vale Royal, and referred to the existing Vale Royal House as Vale Royal Abbey, imagining that the House had once been the abbey itself.' It flourished from 1277 until the Dissolution of the Major Monasteries in 1536

Subsequent to the 1911 and 1958 excavations Vale Royal has acquired a nun buried before the high altar - probably news to the austere Cistercian Abbots, who were generally put into the earth without coffins, often at the threshold of the Abbey Church, so that all who entered would walk on their earthly corruptible remains, and perhaps remember to pray for their incorruptible souls. Over twenty such bodies were found at Vale Royal; only one had a coffin.

Jewish Manchester

We expected to turn up a rich layer of Dybbuk and other phenomena from Manchester's rich Jewish past. Something mournful from the Sephardi Synagogue, moored half way up Cheetham Hill amid the newer Pakistani textile businesses. But nothing. A Golem would have been nice, or even the odd sighting of a secular Marx and Engels, full bearded and frockcoated, researching The Condition of the English Working Class in Manchester's slums.

Non-Haunted Stately Homes

In addition to much book and web research, and some oral interviews, I also wrote to most of the Stately Homes around Manchester, and the following replies were received:

Tatton Old Hall

Tatton Old Hall was probably the site of a manor house from the 1300s, and was occupied until the 1960s, latterly as workmen's cottages. In 660 years it has generated very little in the way of ghostly activity - a presence and some random hair-pulling is about all the present curators will subscribe to. It was investigated by a psychic in 2000 for a television programme. He picked up two girls in Victorian dress in the building's coldspot, and came up with plausible naming for them. He also located a man with dog and gun. Apart from this, nothing. Very reassuring.

Tatton Hall

"No one who lives or works here has a first hand ghost story to tell." Cannot be more categoric than that.

Tabley House

Local people affirmed when the house was opened to the public in 1990 'that it was not haunted in any way, which seemed to be rather a nice change for an old house. They were extraordinarily proud of this.'

However, this statement only applies to this, the third house at Tabley. The second house was a different matter:

> *'The Old Hall is now an old romantic ruin on an island site in Tabley Park. This mediaeval Old Hall was kept up to 1927 when it was left to collapse due to salt brine pumping (which had caused the island to sink). The godson of the then architect told us that he went to the Old Hall with his Godfather, and heard the then owner, Cuthbert Leicester-Warren, give orders that in no way was one of the doors in the Old Hall ever to be opened - it was always to be locked and the Old hall to fall down around it. What was behind it ? What might get out ? Once free could it follow the Leicesters to Tabley House?'*

Smithills Hall & Park

> *'...in the last few years a figure was seen in the chapel one evening after a Friends' social night...when approached, it disappeared and the air in the chapel was very cold....I have not seen anything odd in these buildings.'*

Unpaid Friends' subscription, perhaps.

THE EPITAPH

'Orimur - Morimur - Sequentur qui non præcesserint.'

'We appear, we disappear. They too will soon follow, who have
not already gone before us.'

*Epitaph of Sir Thomas Egerton in Dodleston Church, Cheshire
A.D. 1588*

Peter Portland
All Halloween 2002

A POPULAR CURSE

The Author would like to invite readers to wish a plague of book-worms on whoever stole volumes XXIV and LIV of the Transactions of the Lancashire and Cheshire Antiquarian Society (which appear from the index to contain ghost stories), as well as David Cohen's Guide to Manchester Poltergeists, and sundry other interesting pamphlets from the Manchester Central Library. May their spines crack, may their bindings come apart, and may they be foxed till Doomsday.

We wish them to a warmer place.

Bats, Book and Candle

SELECT BIBLIOGRAPHY & WEBOGRAPHY

SELECT BIBLIOGRAPHY

Alcock, Clara, (1874-75) *'Journal Volume III From July 1874 to May 1875, Clara Alcock, Oakfield Sale'* Manuscript, Manchester Local History Library

Axon, WEA, (1883) *Lancashire Gleanings;* Tubbs Brook and Chrystal, Manchester

Axon, WEA, (1884) *Cheshire Gleanings;* Tubbs Brook and Chrystal, Manchester

Axon, WEA, (1899) *Echoes of Old Lancashire;* William Andrews & Co, London

Baines, Edward, (1888) *History of the County Palatine* and *Duchy of Lancaster*, edited by James Croston;. John Heywood Manchester

Baines, Thomas, (undated) *Lancashire and Cheshire Past and Present*; William MacKenzie London

Barrow, Logie, (1986) *Independent Spirits (Spiritualism and English Plebeians 1850-1910)*, Routledge Kegan Paul, London

Brand, John, (1813), *Observations on Popular Antiquities*, FC & J Rivington et al. London

Camm, Dom Bede, (1910) *Forgotten Shrines*; Macdonald and Evans, London

Conway, Angela, (1995) *Dark Tales of Old Cheshire* by Angela Conway; Sigma Leisure, Wilmslow

Chadderton Historical Society (1999 - no author cited); *The Chadderton Mummy or The Ghost of Birchen Bower; The Strange Tale of Hannah Beswick.*

Earwaker, JP, (1877) *East Cheshire Past and Present*; Two Volumes Printed for the Author, London

Fenton, Edward, (1998), *The Diaries of John Dee*; Day Books, Oxfordshire

Fields, Kenneth,(1998) *Lancashire Magic & Mystery*, Sigma Leisure, Wilmslow

Finucane, RC, (1982), *Appearances of the Dead*; Junction Books, London

Green, Henry, (1869) *Knutsford, Its Traditions and History*; Smith & Elder, London

Guiley, Rosemarie Helen, (1994) *The Guinness Encyclopaedia of Ghosts and Spirits Guinness Publishing*, London

Hardwick, Charles (1872) *Traditions, Superstitions and Folk-Lore, chiefly Lancashire and the North of England*; Republished by EJ Morten, Didsbury 1973

Harland, John, edited (1865) *Ballads and Songs of Lancashire*; Whittaker London

Harland, John, edited (1866) *Lancashire Lyrics*; Whittaker & Co London

Harland, John and Wilkinson TT, (1873) *Lancashire Legends*; LC Gent Manchester

Harland, John and Wilkinson TT, (1882) *Lancashire Folklore*; republished by SR Publishers 1972.

Gregson, Matthew (1867) *Portfolio of Fragments....of the County Palatine and Duchy of Lancaster,* edited by J Harland.. LC Gent, Manchester

Green, Celia and McCreery, Charles (1975 and 1989); *Apparitions* Oxford Institute of Psychophysical Research, Oxford

Hayes, Cliff (undated) *Stories and Tales of Old Manchester;* Aurora Publishing

Hazelgrove, Jenny (2000) *Spiritualism and British Society between the Wars;* Manchester University Press, Manchester

Hole, Christine (1937) *Traditions and Customs of Cheshire.* Republished 1970 by S.R. Publishers

Hough Peter and Randles Jenny (1993) *Mysteries of the Mersey Valley*

Ingham, Albert (1920) *Cheshire, Its Traditions and History, including ... the rise and progress of Freemasonry in this Ancient Province;* Edisbury, Pillans and Wilson

Ingham, John H (1886) *The Haunted House and Family Traditions of Great Britain* Third Edition, WH Allen London

Legh, John (1872) *Lays and Legends of Cheshire;* EJ Morten Didsbury

Lumby, Jonathan (1995) *The Lancashire Witch Craze by Jonathan Lumby,* Carnegie Publishing

McNeil Dodgson, J, (1981) *The Place Names of Cheshire;* English Place Name Society

Middleton,T., (1906) *Legends of Longendale*

Mills MG (1991) *Supernatural Stockport*; Sigma Leisure, Wilmslow

Moss, Fletcher (1898) *Folk Lore*; Privately Published, Manchester

Moss, Fletcher, (1901) *Pilgrimages in Cheshire and Shropshire*, Manchester, Vols 1-6

Mullineux, C. Elsie, (undated) *Ghosts, Little Hulton, Walkden, Worsley*; Streetgate Books

Newton, The Lady (1917) T*he House of Lyme*, Heinemann, London

O'Dea, John (1910) *The Story of the Old Faith in Manchester*; R & T Washbourne, Manchester

Ormerod, George, (1882) *History of Cheshire*, Three Volumes Second Edition London

Pickford, Doug, (1994) *Cheshire, Its Magic and Mystery Sigma*, Wilmslow

Quinlan, Janet, and McGrath, Shaun (1999) *Haunted Sites of Oldham*; Oldham Education and Leisure

Richards, Raymond, (1957) *The Manor of Gawsworth Cheshire;* Ancient Monuments Society, London

Roberts, Robert (1976) *A Ragged Schooling*; Manchester University Press, Manchester

Roby, John (1867) *Traditions of Lancashire by John Roby in 2 volumes*, 4th Edition; George Routledge and Sons, London.

Shercliff, WH (1974) *Wythenshawe*; republished by EJ Morten

Didsbury 1974

Swindells, T, (1907) *Manchester Streets and Manchester*; JE Cornish Manchester

Waugh, Edwin, (undated) *Lancashire Sketches*; John Heywood Manchester

Wever, John (1631), *Funeral Monuments*; Thomas Harper, London

Whitaker, Terence W., (1980) *Lancashire Ghosts and Legends*; Robert Hale 1980

The Catholic Encyclopaedia, Volume II 1907, Published by Robert Appleton Company (Online Edition)

Cheshire Notes and Queries 1890-1906

Manchester Notes and Queries (City News Notes and Queries)

WEBOGRAPHY

Below is a selection of websites which were found useful in researching Around Haunted Manchester. There are many, many more. Web Groups too numerous to mention provide interesting first hand accounts. All sites were running on 13 October 2002. Not all sites specified authorship, so the references below are curtailed to show only page used.

1   GENERAL SITES

For the Boggart as Fairy Tale, and its derivatives see:
http://www.belinus.co.uk/fairytales/English/English041.htm

and also this site which includes 'bargaists'
http://www.belinus.co.uk/folklore/Spencebritishgoblins.htm

For a modern take on the Boggart, see this Brewery site
http://www.boggart-brewery.co.uk/bogglegend.htm

A General Guide to 50 Northern Ghosts:
http://www.mysterymag.com/html/50_northern_ghosts.html

Good Introduction to the modern Horror genre in literature
http://gaslight.mtroyal.ab.ca/superhor.htm

2   PARTICULAR TOWNS and LOCATIONS

Ghosts of Cheshire
http://freespace.virgin.net/martin.lightburn/county/cheshire.htm

'This is weird Cheshire'
http://www.thisischeshire.co.uk/weird/ghosts2.html

A useful guide to the Boggarts in and around Burnley:
http://www.jacknadin2.50megs.com/custom4.html

Clegg Hall, Lancashire: atmospheric photos, and good Lancashire links
http://www.aboutlancs.com/halls/hallcleg.htm

Combermere: not spooky - good images
http://www.users.totalise.co.uk/~craig_thornber/htmlfiles/combermere.html

Gorton: 'Drunken Burgess': a weird and unattributed 18th century poltergeist tale
http://homepage.ntlworld.com/d.a.ratcliffe/lhg/vol6/gorchars.htm

Extraordinary Manchester - includes UFOs
http://www.manchester.com/interactive/extraord.html

Greater Manchester's Mysterious Sites: useful and well written
http://www.mysteriousbritain.co.uk/england/greatermanchester.html

Manchester Association of Paranormal Investigation and Training
http://maxpages.com/mapit

Marple Hall: not spooky - but a good collection of text and images
http://marple-uk.co.uk/Hall1.htm

Ordsall Hall, Salford and Ghost Webcam
http://www.ordsallhall.org/ghostcam/index.html

Archives of the Stockport Ghost Society
http://www.ghost-tours-uk.cwc.net/archives.htm

Skull of Ambrose Barlow at Wardley Hall: marvellous photos.
http://freepages.genealogy.rootsweb.com/~barlow/skull.html

3   SPIRITUALISM
History of Spiritualists National Union
http://www.snu.org.uk/snu.htm

Emma Hardinge Britten: US site with biographical details
http://www.fst.org/hardinge.htm